COPING
WITH

A Learning

Disability

COPING W I T H

A Learning

Disability

Lawrence Clayton, Ph.D. and

Jaydene Morrison

THE ROSEN PUBLISHING GROUP, INC./NEW YORK

Published in 1992, 1995 by The Rosen Publishing Group, Inc.
29 East 21st Street, New York, NY 10010

Revised Edition 1995

Clayton, L. (Lawrence)
      Coping with a learning disability/Lawrence Clayton and Jaydene Morrison.—rev. ed.
            p.   cm.
      Includes bibliographical references and index.
      Summary: Discusses learning disabilities and what can be done to overcome the special problems associated with them.
      ISBN 0-8239-2212-X
      1. Learning disabled teenagers—Education—United States.
      2. Learning disabled teenagers—United States—Family
            relationships. 3. Self-respect. [1. Learning disabilities.]
      I. Morrison, Jaydene.   II. Title.
LC4704.74.C57   1995
371.9—dc20
                                                                            95-39490
                                                                                  CIP
                                                                                    AC

Manufactured in the United States of America

To my daughter, Rebecca,
who inherited all her father's learning disabilities,
for her ability to love and give of herself.

—LC

To my sons
Jay and Mac,
who have taught me more
than any textbook ever could

—JM

Acknowledgments

I want to express my appreciation to the many people who made this book possible: to my coauthor Jaydene Morrison; to Mendy Tidwell for her many hours of editing and typing the manuscript; to Marge Jennings for help in putting together the bibliography; and to my wife, Cathy, and our family, Larry, Rebecca, and Amy, for the hours they spent alone during the writing of this book.

—LC

I wish to express my appreciation primarily to my coauthor Lawrence Clayton and to my dear husband for his patience and endurance during the countless hours I spent writing this book.

—JM

ABOUT THE AUTHORS ◇

Lawrence Clayton became acquainted with learning disabilities through his own, which included auditory figureground disorder (sometimes called discrimination disorder), dyscalculia, and dysgraphia.

He holds a bachelor's degree (summa cum laude) from Texas Wesleyan College, a master's degree from Texas Christian University, and a doctorate from Texas Woman's University.

Since 1971 Dr. Clayton has specialized in treating children, youth, and families as an ordained minister, clinical marriage and family therapist, and certified drug and alcohol counselor. He founded and directs the Oklahoma Family Institute in Oklahoma City. He is an Approved Supervisor for the American Association for Marriage and Family Therapy and President of the Certification Board for Drug and Alcohol Counselors.

Dr. Clayton is the author of *Assessment and Management of the Suicidal Adolescent, Coping with Depression, Coping with Being Gifted*, and *Careers in Psychology*. He serves as an associate editor for the journal *Family Perspective*.

Dr. Clayton lives with his wife, Cathy, and children, Rebecca, Larry, and Amy, in Piedmont, Oklahoma.

Jaydene Morrison is a native-born Oklahoman of pioneer stock. Her great-grandfather was a country doctor who made the Cherokee Strip Run of 1893. Holder of eight teaching certificates, she is a Nationally Certified Counselor and School Psychologist, holding a master's degree from Oklahoma State University. She is also a Licensed Professional Counselor.

She practices biofeedback and serves as a consultant for Dr. Lawrence Clayton. She also works with the Oklahoma City Public School System, where she is involved with identification of disabled students and works with staff and students involving psychological services.

She is presently head of the Diaconate in her church.

She has two grown sons, Jay and Mac. She lives with her husband, Dr. Mike, a junior college biology and physiology instructor; Terrible Termite, her toy French poodle, and Cali, her calico cat.

Contents

CHAPTER 1

"So, I've Got a Learning Disability"

They say I have a what? There's nothing wrong with me—or is there? Why does everyone look at me as if I'm weird? Do they think I'm stupid?

Many people do think learning disabled people are dumb. Nothing could be further from the truth. Would you call Albert Einstein, Thomas Edison, or Steven Spielberg stupid? These people are considered learning disabled. Albert Einstein flunked math in high school yet developed a theory of relativity that other mathematicians couldn't understand. Thomas Edison's mother took him out of school because his teachers thought he was retarded. She taught him herself at home, and he later invented the light bulb and the telephone. Even though school work was difficult and boring for him, Steven Spielberg made the most of his talents to become one of the most successful movie makers in the world.

Having a learning disability does not mean that you are stupid. It means that you are as smart as anyone else but that your brain works differently from most people's brains. Certain functions of your brain do not respond to traditional methods of teaching and need special attention that is not provided in a typical classroom. It is called special education because it is provided by specially trained teachers who help activate your brain in special classes.

The important thing to remember about a learning disability is that having one often means that you have an exceptional, offsetting, *capability*.

John and Phil

John and Phil are in the same school. John is the quiet one who used to worry his parents because he was so afraid of strangers and new situations. He is not much interested in sports, and it took him all summer to learn to swim. He has always been very sensitive to criticism and often cries if he is told to keep trying. Phil is his best friend, but the two could not be more different. Phil is very athletic. He is always the first to be chosen when teams are being picked. He is expressive and funny and extremely popular. In the classroom, however, there are more differences. John has almost finished reading *Gulliver's Travels*, whereas Phil, who has trouble reading, is struggling to get through a primer.

Einstein once said, "Intelligence is not the ability to store information but to know where to find it." Special education teachers help you to "rewire your brain" so you can find that information. In some cases, especially if you have more than one disability, this can take time, but the help of a special education teacher is important in overcoming a learning disability.

Special education classes are designed to work with your regular class schedule. In the mornings you go to your usual classes, and in the afternoons you spend an hour or two with your special education teacher. If your school does not offer classes that suit your needs, you may commute to another school for your afternoon sessions. Typically, most students notice an improvement within months after starting special education.

IDENTIFYING YOUR LEARNING DISABILITY

The doctor says you have a learning disability but your school counselor says you don't? That is not unusual. There are many ways of testing and evaluating a person's learning capabilities, and frequently two sources disagree. If you or your family have any doubts about an evaluation, get another opinion. Most often, teachers refer students with learning problems to specialists who identify the problem and recommend a special education program. Doctors and psychologists describe learning disabilities in clinical terms. These are some of the most common learning disabilities and their clinical names:

Developmental arithmetic disorder (sometimes called **dyscalculia**). In this disability learning occurs at a normal rate except in mathematics. Persons may be failing math but be far ahead of the rest of the class in history or English. Multiplication can be extremely difficult for these students and higher math almost impossible without specialized training and use of a calculator.

Developmental expressive writing disorder. This disability affects a person's composition and writing skills. He or she is slow to learn how to write without making grammatical, punctuation, and spelling errors.

Developmental reading disorder. Persons with this disability are behind in reading, both silent and oral. They often combine two or more words into one, using the first half of one word with the second half of another. Often words are omitted entirely. The result is diffculty in understanding and retaining what has been read.

Developmental articulation disorder. Persons with this disorder sound as if they are using baby talk. They are far behind in their ability to articulate and may utter sounds and syllables that have no meaning to the listener. They also may omit or substitute certain sounds. For example, they may say, "I thwew a wock at the gawage window."

Developmental expressive language disorder. In this disability, a person is behind in oral communication skills. The disorder makes it hard to learn new words and expand the vocabulary. With few words from which to choose, he or she might say "open the gate" when "open the refrigerator door" is the intended message. The condition can be so severe that the person cannot speak at all.

Developmental receptive disorder. This disability causes people to have difficulty understanding other people's speech. They do not recognize spoken words even if they are familiar with their meaning and appearance on paper.

Attention-deficit disorder. This disability affects a person's concentration. People with this disorder tend to daydream and are easily distracted. They also act impulsively and spontaneously.

Attention-deficit hyperactivity disorder. Persons with this disorder have difficulty paying attention plus inability to sit still. They fidget, blurt out answers to questions, fail to wait their turn, and are impatient with others.

Cluttering disorder. Persons with this disorder alternate between a rapid and slow pace while speaking. They also talk in a singsong manner.

Sequencing disorder. Persons with this disability tend to reverse the order of words and numbers. The phone number 405-787-0007 may come out 504-878-7000. A phrase like "twenty-two rifle" may be said "two-renty tifle." The transpositions happen in both speech and writing.

Tracking disorder. This disability causes difficulty in following an object, whether a ball or an airplane. It also causes difficulty staying on the same line in reading. The person may read:

Lillian ran as fast as she could to help her mother, but it seemed as if she couldn't run fast enough.

as:

Lillian ran as fast as she couldn't run fast enough.

Fine motor skills disorder (often called **dysgraphia**). Persons with this disability are usually very good with gross motor (large muscle) skills. They may be excellent basketball players or weight lifters. They have trouble with fine muscle movements such as writing, drawing, sewing, or typing. They may fail to complete math assignments, not because they have difficulty understanding the math but because writing down the problems exhausts them. Written work is tiresome and boring to them.

Auditory figureground disorder (often called **discrimination disorder**). Persons with this disability have trouble separating out competing sounds. For example, a student listening to a teacher while a radio plays outside may not be able to hear the teacher's speech clearly; it becomes garbled and confused.

Visual figureground disorder. This disability is similar to auditory figureground disorder but affects vision instead of sound. The images on a page compete and tend to become blurry or abstract. A person with this disorder may have trouble locating a particular tool in a box of tools or finding a friend in a crowd of people.

Visual Closure Disorder. Persons with this disability have trouble finishing an incomplete visual image. If they see a neon sign that is partly burned out, it may be hard for them to decipher the message. For example, "H lida Inn" may not be understood to read "Holiday Inn."

Auditory Closure Disorder. This is like visual closure disorder but with hearing. The listener is unable to hear every word that is said and is unable to fill in the gaps. Suppose a person with this disorder was listening to this announcement on a faulty PA system: "Tomorrow is a very impor**** day. When you get to school you *ust fir** go to room 2*5 to get your registrat*** forms." The intended message may not be assimilated as: "Tomorrow is a very important day. When you get to school you must first go to room 205 to get your registration forms."

Alexia, or **visual aphasia,** or **word-blindness disorder.** Under any of its names, this disorder interferes with the association process or recognition that is involved in reading. The letters most commonly confused are *b* and *d* and *p* and *q*. The principal difference between this and developmental reading disorder is that developmental disorders may be caused by immaturity. People develop on different time lines. Research has shown that boys at the age of five are about six months behind girls of the same chronological age. Reversals of developmental disorders are common at the age of eight or nine, whereas alexia may persist into and through the pubescent years.

Agraphia or **Dysgraphia.** This disability is similar to visual aphasia except that it involves writing the letters *b* and *d* and *p* and *q* instead of reading them. It differs from developmental expressive writing disorder in that the latter may be caused by immaturity and is likely to diminish in severity or disappear entirely at the onset of puberty. Like alexia, agraphia is likely to persist beyond puberty.

Dyslexia. Dyslexia refers to most disabilities that interfere with normal reading and writing, including the disabilities above. Dyslexic people often reverse the order of numbers and letters. They may have orientation difficulties and read from right to left instead of left to right.

Perseveration Disorder. Persons with this disability have difficulty stopping a task even though it is finished. They also have trouble switching from one concept or line of thought to another. For instance, a student doing a set of math problems may do four addition problems correctly, then continue to add the next three multiplication problems.

Left to right orientation disorder. Persons with this disability tend to confuse their right and left.

On the whole, attention deficit-hyperactivity disorder (ADHD) and dyslexia are the most commonly diagnosed learning disabilities. Experts on ADHD say it afflicts as many as 3.5 million American youngsters, or up to 5 percent of Americans under the age of 18. It is two to three times more likely to be diagnosed in boys than girls. A decade ago doctors believed that the symptoms of ADHD diminished with maturity. Now it is one of the fastest growing diagnostic categories for adults. Specialists estimate that one third to two thirds of ADHD kids continue to shown signs of the disorder as adults. Experts also note that ADHD tends to run in families. Estimates show that 40 percent of kids with ADHD have a parent with the disability and 35 percent are likely to have a sibling with the trait.

Once a person is diagnosed with a learning disability, he or she is likely to be tested to determine the extent of the disability. Often the disability has only a slight effect on learning and is overcome with minimal special education. If the disability severely interferes with learning and sets the person far behind his or her age group, he or she may be entitled to financial assistance from the government. The Department of Education for each state has criteria for defining a "significant discrepancy" in education level. Most states lean toward an "inclusion" program whereby learning disabled students receive special attention as part of the school's regular curriculum.

The tests that help define the severity of a learning disability can be fun. There are no grades, so passing or failing is not a concern. The doctors may have puzzles for you to work, blocks to play with, or pictures to look at. These things will help identify if you perceive things upside-down or backward. Your academic level will be tested in seven areas that are established by the federal government: oral expression, listening, written expression, basic reading skills, reading comprehension, math calculation, and math reasoning. The tests can be affected by many factors such as health, amount of sleep, anxiety level, and mood. If you're not feeling yourself the day of your testing, reschedule the appointment for another day.

Billy

Billy was very excited to go back to school and tried very hard in all his classes, but by the time the semester was half over he was well behind and in some classes actually failing. Billy found it difficult to pay attention and kept wanting to get up from his seat. He was easily distracted by the other kids and by things he saw that he wanted to touch or play with. His teachers didn't make any sense to him, and it made him cry when they insisted that he keep trying to complete his work when he simply couldn't. One day a school counselor told him that tomorrow he was going to be given some tests. She told him where to go and when, but she didn't say what the tests were for. Billy had even more trouble concentrating that afternoon. He kept wondering about the tests. What did he need to study?

At home, Billy was depressed. He couldn't relax, and

he couldn't do his homework. He tried to sleep but tossed and turned all night and woke up weary. He was running late, so he skipped breakfast.

When the counselor came to take him to the testing room, Billy was nervous and his stomach ached. He was told to sit at a table where there were several objects and a lot of pictures. Billy tried to pay attention to the instructions and the questions that he was asked, but he was hungry and sleepy. He could not wait for the session to end.

A few days later, the counselor called Billy again and said she wanted to share the test results with him and his parents. The scores were very low. Billy's parents were upset. The counselor remarked that the scores were much lower than she would have expected and asked Billy if he was having a bad day when he took the tests. "Bad day?" Billy said. "It was the worst!"

It was decided that Billy would retake the tests the next week. The new results were much better, but they revealed that Billy had attention deficit-hyperactivity disorder and a form of dyslexia. Billy was relieved to know that other kids had the same trouble he did, and he couldn't wait to start the special education classes that the counselor said would help him.

In four months, Billy had caught up with his classmates. He still felt the urge to get out of his seat and move around, but he was able to concentrate better and understand more. Billy's grades improved too, and he was determined to get an A before the year was over.

We have long known that your real ability can be above the marks you receive on tests. We also know that it can be below them. Your real ability and knowledge can also increase with experience and with the things you learn as time goes by. In fact, you should be getting smarter every day of your life.

CHAPTER 2

Areas of Learning

Disabilities

According to the Learning Disabilities Association of America, if a youngster consistently demonstrates a number of these signs, it may mean that he or she should be referred to a specialist to be tested for a learning disability.

Watch for the person who:

- is disorganized,
- is easily distracted,
- has poor attention span,
- overreacts to noise,
- doesn't enjoy being read to,
- has poor eye-to-hand coordination,
- can't make sense of what he or she hears,
- uses words inappropriately,
- has a limited vocabulary,
- is unable to follow simple instructions,

- sometimes has poor emotional control,
- has difficulty remembering or understanding sequences
- chooses younger playmates or prefers solitary play.

Psychologists believe that behaviors like these are signs of disabilities in one or more basic mental processes. These basic areas are: oral expression, listening, written expression, reading skills, reading comprehension, math calculation, and math reasoning.

Oral Expression

Oral expression is the measure of how you understand information and how you tell it to others. For example, you might be asked to describe a woman's purse. How many things can you say about a purse?

Jane

Jane's grades were good in reading, spelling, and math, but she could never explain things she knew to anyone else. Jane was very shy and seldom talked to her friends. At home she stayed in her room most of the time and did not associate with her brother and sister. Jane thought her sister was prettier and smarter than she. She spent her time studying so she could make better grades than her sister or brother, but try as hard as she could she just made Cs. Her sister made As and her brother made Bs.

Jane often overheard her parents referring to her as "poor Jane." Last year her English teacher had suggested that she be tested to see if she had a learning disability. Jane begged her mother not to agree to the test; she was secretly afraid they would all find out how stupid she was.

Jane's mother was reluctant to sign the papers, but Mrs. James, the English teacher, finally persuaded her to do it.

The night before the tests Jane tossed and turned all night. She was terrified the next morning when she met with the speech pathologist and then the psychometrist. They visited with her separately, and before she knew it she was enjoying working with them.

When she got home, her parents and her sister all wanted to know what she had been asked. Jane just said, "Oh, a bunch of questions and things to read and do."

The next day she asked Mrs. James what the tests showed, but the teacher said the results would take about two weeks. That seemed like forever to Jane, but finally her parents received a letter from the school asking them to come for a meeting with the "team" to discuss the test results. Jane asked to go to the meeting. Her mother and father talked it over and decided to let her go. Jane was surprised to see that the "team" was the school principal, Mrs. James, the speech pathologist, the psychometrist, and a special education teacher.

First the psychometrist explained the test results. She said that Jane was really smart and that her academic scores were on grade level. Her oral expression score was far below grade level and her ability level. Jane had not been able to talk about things on the level that they expected of her.

The team recommended that Jane be placed in the special education class for help in oral expression. (In some schools the speech pathologist works with oral expression.) They explained that they would meet again in a year to assess Jane's progress and that she would be tested again in three years unless the parents or teachers requested the tests sooner.

Listening Comprehension

Listening is a measure of how well you remember what you are told. The tests measure your ability to remember things in order and repeat them to the examiner. You are asked to repeat numbers and sentences exactly as they were said to you. The examiner may read you a story and ask you questions about it.

Some people have trouble remembering what people tell them. My grandmother used to say it just goes in one ear and out the other. Some of these problems we never outgrow; we just learn to cope with them. One of the authors has a form of listening or discrimination disorder, technically known as auditory figureground. Although most tests do not cover this specific disorder, it can interfere with listening ability. It involves hearing several different voices or sounds at once and trying to make sense out of them. Last week Dr. C. was driving with his wife and daughter. Over the sound of the car radio his wife said, "I found the best recipe to try for dinner tonight. Do you like sautéd onions?" At the same time his daughter was telling about her day in school. "Daddy, I met the cutest boy. I was walking down the hall and he came up and said, 'Hi'. I couldn't think of anything to say to him." With everyone talking at once, Dr. C. was unable to process any of the information. He turned off the radio and asked them to take turns talking to him.

Written Expression

Written expression is a measure of your ability to spell words, use punctuation and capitalization, and understand word usage, as for instance formation of plurals.

Charles

When Charles wrote words, the letters tended to get jumbled up. He could never remember if you spelled it *read* or *raed*; they seemed to him to sound the same. His grades were all right in first grade, where there was little spelling. In second grade he made Ds and Fs. His mother made him write spelling words every night until he hated to come home from school. By third grade Charles was mad at his teacher and his mother. His mother finally discussed the problem with the teacher, who suggested referring Charles for testing. The test results showed that he was far behind his ability level in spelling, word usage, punctuation, and capitalization. His mother met with the school team (school principal, classroom teacher, psychometrist, and special education teacher), and it was decided to get him some help in special education.

Each year his special education teacher sets goals to help him get closer to his grade level and ability level. At first his classroom teacher asked him to learn five spelling words a week, and he worked on those words in special education class. He was very proud when he found that he could make As in spelling. As he improved he was given more and more words. By hard work he was able to keep his grades up. His special education teacher also helped him with plurals and other forms of speech, punctuation, and capitalization.

When Charles was in sixth grade he was retested. The scores showed that he had made dramatic improvement, but his parents and teachers decided to keep him in special education, as he was still behind. In eighth grade his teacher suggested that he be retested even though the three years for reevaluation were not up. The results showed that Charles was working at grade level. It was a happy time for Charles and his family.

Basic Reading Skills/Reading Comprehension

The test for basic reading skills requires you to pronounce words. The test for reading comprehension measures your ability to understand the words you read. Most tests ask you to fill in a missing word in a story:"Mary walks on the sidewalk between lots of tall buildings. She enjoys her walks in the big _____." As you probably guessed, the word *city* goes in the blank.

Jason

Jason had trouble writing words, reading words, and understanding what they meant. When he was in first grade his teacher suggested that he be tested because he was having too many problems. His mother signed the papers, but the family moved before he was tested. The teacher at the new school said he was immature and should be kept in the first grade the next year. Jason felt he must be really dumb to be held back. His dad assured him that it was all right; in fact neither his dad nor his mother had finished high school. The next year in first grade was much better, but the end of the year got harder. Second grade started off pretty well but began getting hard in the middle of the year.

His parents moved again. Jason was really behind the kids in the new school. They all treated him as if he were stupid. The work got harder and harder. The teacher spoke to Jason's mother about holding him back, and his mother told her that his first-grade teachers had wanted him tested. The teacher arranged for the testing, but again his parents moved.

By that time it was May and only a few weeks until school would be out. His parents did not enter him in the new school, and he had a delightful summer.

In September his mother took him to the new school and told the teachers that he was in third grade. He was totally lost. He came home from school every afternoon and cried. He felt so stupid. He couldn't do the work the other kids were doing. Finally the school notified his mother that Jason's records had come from his previous school and he had never been passed to third grade. They said he would have to repeat second grade.

Jason cried all that night and told his parents he would never go to that school again. His folks decided just to move again. Enrolled in the third grade at the new school, things were just the same. Jason couldn't understand what they were reading.

By this time Jason knew he had to be the stupidest kid in town, but he was also learning how to keep people from knowing how stupid he was. He acted mean and scared all the other kids. He acted mean to the teacher. That meant that he spent most of his time in the principal's office and didn't have to do his work. The principal suggested to his mother that he be tested for a learning disability. Again his mother signed the paper.

The psychometrist came to the school the next week and tested Jason before his parents could move. When they were told the test results they said, "Hey Jason, where'd you get all your smarts? The school says you are really smart but just have trouble with spelling and reading."

Jason was put in special education for written expression, basic reading skills, and reading comprehension. He was surprised to find that he stayed in his regular room and just went for part of the day to a "Resource Room" for help in reading, spelling, word usage, punctuation, and capitalization. Several of his friends went there too. The special education teacher helped him learn to pronounce words and to understand what they meant in sentences. His classroom teacher changed the material she was using with him. All at once school became a lot more fun. Jason didn't feel so much like hitting the other kids. The teacher even seemed nicer. Just as things were starting to turn around for him, his folks decided to move. However, his teacher gave his parents a lot of papers to take to the new school.

There he was enrolled in the special classes as well as his regular classroom. Jason found out that the government requires all school systems to go by those papers, which are called an IEP (individualized education program).

Life was going great for Jason. His parents made lots of moves over the next few years, but they always took the IEP papers with them. In eighth and ninth grade the work got really hard. Without the special help, he would have given up and dropped out of school.

Jason was able to complete the tenth grade. His parents were expecting him to quit, and he was secretly thinking about it. During his junior year he did decide to drop out, even though things were going well. His vocational teacher (shop teacher) began talking to him about going on to votech school or college. Jason wasn't interested, but his teacher didn't give up. He took Jason to visit a votech school and a junior college. Jason became interested enough to ask questions, and the more questions he asked, the more he was interested. He asked, "Do you really think I could do it? No one in my family has even completed high school." His teacher encouraged him to try.

The day Jason graduated from high school his mother, dad, grandmother, grandfather, uncles, aunts, and all of their kids came to see the first one in their family

graduate from high school. In the middle of the cere-
monies the principal asked Jason to step forward and
presented him with a scholarship to a junior college. The
principal announced that Jason had been chosen the
outstanding student of the graduating class because he
had worked the hardest and made the most progress of
any student over the last two years. Jason was struggling
hard to hold back tears. He looked out in the audience
and saw his mother and father both crying. The pride that
he saw in their eyes and in the eyes of all his relatives was
unbelievable. He couldn't help it; tears slipped down his
cheeks as he shook hands with the principal.

Today you will find Jason strolling across the campus at
junior college. The college has special help for learning
disabled students. The counseling office also helped him
get a part-time job to help pay his educational expenses.

Math Calculation/Math Reasoning

The math calculation test has problems in addition, sub-
traction, multiplication, division, and fractions. You do
only the problems you know how to do. With math comprehension, the examiner may read math problems to you
and ask you to give the answer. You may use paper and
pencil to figure on if you wish.

Richard

Richard was a whiz at reading. In fact, he was the best
reader in his class. He was able to add and subtract. In
the third grade, however, the class started multiplication,
which was difficult for him. In fourth grade he started
bringing home Ds and Fs in arithmetic, and his teacher
was talking about holding him back. Richard's mother

saw a television program about students with learning disabilities and asked his teacher if that could be his problem. The teacher said she didn't think so, but she offered to arrange to have him tested. His mother signed the papers.

Richard didn't want to be tested, but he had given up and was ready to try anything. The test results showed that his mother was right: He did meet the qualifications for special help in learning disabilities in both math calculation and math comprehension. He has a condition called dyscalculia. In fifth grade his math teacher allowed him to use a calculator. With the combination of his special education class and the use of his calculator, Richard is doing great. His teacher expects him to be transferred out of special education next year.

CHAPTER 3

Personal Reactions

The emotional consequences of being learning disabled are extremely varied. They range from "So what?" to "My life is ruined" to "This is just another attempt of the school system to get me!"

Your emotional reaction is largely determined by one or more of nine factors: (1) how long it was before your learning disability was discovered; (2) how serious your disability is; (3) how easily it can be compensated for; (4) whether or not your compensation strategy opens you up to ridicule; (5) how other kids relate to you because of your disability; (6) how the teacher relates to you; (7) the written and unwritten policies of the school; (8) how your family react; and (9) how you react.

One of the most important elements is how long it was before your learning disability was diagnosed. Some teenagers were diagnosed as soon as they started school, so they have been working on coping strategies for years, often with the help of parents and teachers.

*   *   *

Barbara Ann was a sharp, bright-eyed little girl. Her parents could always spot her in a group of children because she was the one who would be laughing. Strangers often commented on what a happy child she was. Then she started kindergarten. By the Christmas break the light had gone out of her eyes. One day when her father started to take her to school Barbara Ann sat down on the steps and refused to budge. "I hate school," she screamed. Her father, a child psychologist, couldn't figure out what had happened to his happy little girl. No matter what he did, he could not convince Barbara Ann that she needed to go to school.

Her father referred Barbara Ann to a fellow child psychologist for testing and discovered that she was learning disabled. She had an auditory figureground disorder. When confronted with competing sounds like the teacher talking and another child shuffling papers, Barbara Ann could understand nothing. It just got all mixed up in her head. The psychologist told Barbara Ann's father that several things could be done to help. First, she should be placed at the front of the class, as near the teacher as possible; second, the teacher could be provided with a small microphone and Barbara Ann be given a small headset receiver, which would allow the teacher to speak directly to the child; and third, Barbara Ann should do her homework in the quietest room in the house to cut down on distractions.

Barbara Ann's parents and teacher followed these recommendations. By the time she was twelve she was not only performing as well as her peers in most subjects but was well ahead of them in history and English.

Others are not so fortunate. Their learning disabilities are not diagnosed until they are well into high school or in college.

Jonas was twenty-three years old. He had completed college and was halfway through a master's degree in psychology and doing his clinical internship at a mental health clinic. Once a month Jonas and the other interns were assigned a ten-page paper by the director of the program. Jonas's first paper was near perfect; every word was spelled correctly, and the grammar was faultless. Jonas's second paper was, as his clinical director said, "one of the worst messes I've ever seen." The director called his professor at college to say, "These two papers are simply not the work of the same individual." In short, he was accusing Jonas of plagiarism, of copying some-one else's work for his first paper. His professor, after reading the paper, agreed. Jonas was about to be ex-pelled when he went to the college counselor because he was depressed.

After hearing his story, the counselor tested Jonas for learning disabilities. What he discovered astounded everyone: Jonas was dyslexic. He saw words backwards— *Australia* looked like *ailartsuA*.

Jonas thought all people saw words backwards. When he had plenty of time he simply went through his work and reversed the order of every word that looked correct to him. When he was under stress or pressed for time, however, he often missed some words. He also mixed up commas and periods. The result was that his second paper was indeed "a mess."

When the professor and clinical director understood the problem, they made adjustments in Jonas's schedule that allowed him extra time to complete written assignments.

His response was to break down crying, saying, "All my life I've felt stupid. Other kids seemed to get good grades without even trying, and it took me all night to write one paper." When the counselor heard this, he gave Jonas an intellegence test that took his learning disability into consideration. Everyone was surprised once more when the test revealed that his IQ was 168—several points above genius level. Jonas was a very smart person who was spending all his time trying to compensate for his learning disability.

Jonas was clearly an exception. Imagine what would have happened to him if he had had only an average IQ. He probably would never have finished high school.

Another important factor is how seriously disabled you are. Some people have only one learning disability whereas others have several. Obviously someone with multiple learning disabilities will have a harder time adjusting.

Mecole had a problem with fine motor skills. Writing was very difficult for her; in fact, it exhausted her. (Fine motor skills problems are typical of people who have suffered from anoxia—oxygen deprivation of the brain. These people perhaps did not breathe immediately after birth or suffered a period of unconsciousness at some time later in life.) When Mecole's problem was discovered by her teacher, he made several adjustments to his class requirements. Mecole was allowed to dictate written assignments into a recorder. She also did not have to copy a whole page of math problems; the teacher wrote them for her, and she could simply write the answers. Almost overnight Mecole's grades went from Ds and Fs to As and Bs.

Mark, however, has both a tracking problem and an expressive disorder. Because of the tracking disorder Mark cannot stay on the same line when reading. He often begins one line and finishes another. This makes books seem incomprehensible to him. Because of the expressive disorder Mark's brain understands information very well, but he is unable to tell others what he knows. For instance, when he wanted to refer to a substitute teacher his class had, he called her "the pink lady," meaning that she wore a pink dress. Mark's tracking problem can be helped by placing a ruler under each line as he reads. His second problem, the expressive disorder, will take years to correct with the help of a trained speech pathologist.

Another important issue is how easy it is to compensate for your particular learning disability. Some disabilities are very easily adjusted to; others are extremely difficult.

Maylene was unable to focus on objects with both eyes. Her eyes actually looked at two separate points in front of her; as a matter of fact, the farther away an object was, the farther apart were the two points. The school nurse discovered the problem and referred Maylene to an optometrist. After an examination, the optometrist ordered glasses with lenses that allowed Maylene to focus correctly.

*   *   *

Alicia has difficulty sitting still. She squirms constantly and can hardly wait her turn in the cafeteria line. She frequently blurts out answers to questions before the speaker has finished asking them. She often "speed talks," running sentences together. She seldom stops long enough to hear what other people are saying. Alicia loses almost anything, from a pencil to a library book to a homework assignment. But most of all, she has difficulty paying attention. This is a condition called attention-deficit disorder with hyperactivity (ADD).

Alicia's parents have tried everything. They've had her in therapy with a learning disorder specialist for years. They've tried Ritalin, a drug that is sometimes effective in controlling hyperactivity and in smaller doses in controlling attention problems. Alicia had an allergic reaction to Ritalin. They have tried structuring her every waking minute. In desperation they even tried Great-aunt Alice's home remedy for kids with "ants in their pants," a concoction of gypsum root tea and cottage cheese. Nothing worked except the tea, which succeeded in slowing Alicia down only until she got over her nausea. They hope that Alicia will "grow out of it." Most hyperactive children do grow out of it when they reach puberty; those who don't probably never will.

One of the major emotional impacts of a learning disorder is whether or not attempts to compensate bring ridicule from one's peers. The more bizarre the compensation technique, the more ridicule.

Micah had a sequencing disorder that caused him to reverse the order of numbers and letters. When he wrote *final* it might come out *finla*. He also mixed up terms like "hot water heater" so it came out "wot hater heater." Most of his friends and Micah himself found this very funny. A lot of good-natured joking and teasing resulted.

Gary, however, was not so fortunate. His disability was such that it opened him up to much ridicule from other teenagers. Even adults sometimes considered him weird.

Gary had a developmental articulation disorder, which involves frequent substitution or omission of speech sounds, making the speaker seem to be talking baby talk. This disorder has nothing to do with intelligence level, but it causes the person to appear very immature.

Developmental articulation disorder is one of the hardest disabilities to overcome. While the rest of the brain has developed at a normal, or even faster than normal, rate, the part that controls articulation has not. It is often many years behind, and in some cases it never catches up. Treatment by a speech pathologist or therapist is the most successful means of help. It also requires much practice. The difficulty is that the more Gary talks, the more other teenagers make fun of him. Gary is becoming more and more reluctant to speak in public, and he absolutely dreads speech class. All of his grades are slipping, and he is becoming more and more withdrawn. His teacher is concerned that he may be considering suicide. She has asked for a conference with his parents and intends to suggest that Gary have intensive psychotherapy.

Closely related to the issue of ridicule is the question of how other teenagers respond to finding out that you are learning disabled. Once again there are a variety of responses. Some people will try to help while others will put you down. Some will think you are incompetent, while others think you have a relatively small problem that can be overcome with ease. Let us look at two case histories of teenagers with exactly the same learning disability.

Jeremy had a developmental language disorder, in which everything but language develops at a normal rate. He was very good in science and math. In fact, for five years he placed in the top three teenagers at the State Science Fair. Although he knew a lot, however, Jeremy had tremendous trouble talking. His friends responded by giving him extra time to answer when they asked questions. They also made it a point not to interrupt when he paused in mid-sentence to think how to complete his sentence. In addition, they valued Jeremy's knowledge of math and science and let him know that they did. They often asked his help on homework. Jeremy came through with his self-image intact.

Merissa, however, was not so fortunate. She too had a developmental language disorder, but her schoolmates responded very differently from Jeremy's. One day when Merissa was seven years old she was late getting ready for school. In fact, the bus had to wait for her. When she got on and started down the aisle looking for a seat, the other kids started screaming, "Get back, retard!" and "Don't let the retard touch you, she's contagious." Merissa at first tried to respond, but she was too upset. She just stood there and cried. At school the kids continued to call her "retard"—a name that has been with her ever since. She has been excluded from most school relationships. She is never invited to any of her schoolmates' birthday parties, and last year when she was twelve no one at all showed up for her party. Despite the fact that Merissa has a very high IQ, all this has really gotten to her. She has become more and more withdrawn. Her counselor recently told her parents that the cruelty of her peers has seriously damaged her self-esteem and that it may take years of counseling to help her.

It is also important to consider how your teacher responds to you as a learning disabled person. Some teachers go out of their way to make life miserable, whereas others do everything in their power to help.

Jonathan has a developmental arithmetic disorder, in which everything develops at a normal, even above normal, rate, but mathematics abilities lag far behind. Jonathan's math teacher, Mr. Musser, doesn't believe in learning disorders; he thinks Jonathan is just lazy. Jonathan's counselor and his parents have tried to explain learning disorders to Mr. Musser, to no avail. He says, "I understand that some kids just don't have what it takes." When Jonathan was struggling with a problem and asked for his help, he said, "I think the main problem is that you are intellectually lazy. I'm going to stay on you till you get it. I'm willing to scream at you every class period for the rest of this year, if necessary, but you will get it." Jonathan had already disliked math at the beginning of the year. Now he hates it. His parents are not certain what steps to take, but they are certain that Mr. Musser's attitude is hurting, not helping, Jonathan.

Susanne also had a developmental arithmetic disorder. Her teacher, Mrs. Porter, was very supportive. As a child, Mrs. Porter had had a learning disorder, which she had been able to overcome with much help from her teachers. As a result, she had a soft spot in her heart for kids who struggled with learning disorders. When Susanne had worked as hard as she could and still couldn't understand a problem, Mrs. Porter would say, "Honey, I understand. It can be really frustrating to work as hard as you do and still not catch on. Let me show you a trick I learned when I was your age." The nice part was that when Mrs. Porter said, "I understand," she really did understand. That made Susanne feel both understood and cared for. It also motivated her to work even harder. "After all," she told her friends, "if Mrs. Porter could overcome a learning disability, so can I."

One of the most surprising, and yet very important, factors is how the school system deals with learning disabled persons. In some school systems the principal and administration refer privately to special education classes as "collections of boneheads." Although such an attitude would never be expressed in public, it can spread through a school like a plague. As a result teenagers in special education classes and their teachers tend to be looked down on by their peers. You can feel the impact of such a negative attitude, but it is hard to determine its source.

Other schools take pride in the quality of their special education programs. That attitude also spreads through a school system. As a result students and teachers receive a lot of positive attention and feel special and cared for.

Obviously one of the major ingredients in your emotional reaction to being learning disabled is how your family responded to the fact. We discuss family responses at length in Chapter 4.

When you come right down to it, the single most important factor in adjusting to the knowledge that you are learning disabled is your own reaction. Although it is certainly affected by the other issues discussed in this chapter, this is the bottom line. Some people respond to finding out that they have a learning disability by falling apart, becoming depressed, and feeling hopeless. Others respond by deciding to do whatever is necessary to deal with the problem. Here are case studies of two teenagers who have the same learning disorder but responded in quite different ways.

Phyllis was diagnosed as a clutterer. In cluttering the rate of speech is not constant. The speaker talks very fast, then very slowly, then very fast again. He or she also talks in a singsong manner.

When Phyllis was told that she had a disorder called cluttering, it confirmed her worst fears. She had long been afraid that she was insane. Even though her counselor explained over and over that having a learning disability did not mean you were crazy, Phyllis did not believe him. She was convinced that he was only trying to save her feelings. As a result she made excuses to avoid going to see him. She also refused to practice as he told her to do, believing that it would only show people how crazy she was. Her resistance caused Phyllis to suffer with her disability years longer than necessary. She also suffered severe damage to her already fragile self-esteem.

Steven responded to the information with relief. Before finding out that there was both a name and a treatment for his problem, he too had worried that he might be insane. Despite knowing exactly what he wanted to say, when he opened his mouth all that came out sounded like nonsense. It was very frustrating. But now that Steven knew what the problem was, he had something that he could really fight. And fight he did! He attended speech therapy every day for a while, and what he learned he practiced at home. He got his parents and sister to help him practice. In fact, he practiced so much that his parents often had to stop him because it was well past his bedtime. As a result, Steven overcame his disability with lightning speed. Today he has no noticeable speech problem.

Some people who are diagnosed with a learning disability respond by going into a serious depression. If that has happened to you, you will probably need help from a professional. The symptoms of depression are tearfulness, drug or alcohol abuse, feelings of guilt, a negative attitude, low self-esteem, difficulty in concentrating, a feeling of hopelessness and helplessness, a sudden drop in grades, thoughts of death and suicide, withdrawal from friends, anger, sadness, difficulty in making decisions, and loss of interest in appearance. If you are aware of any four of these symptoms, it is time to get the help of a trained counselor. To find out how to get the help you need, see Chapter 9.

It is important to remember that all of the nine factors in your emotional reaction have an impact on your self-image—how you see yourself.

Almost all learning disabled teenagers have had their feelings hurt repeatedly by parents, teachers, and friends. Sometimes the hurt is intentional, sometimes not. But most of you learn to respond to life by isolating yourselves from others, even though you often desperately want to be included. You also become afraid to answer questions because of possible ridicule.

You feel different from others, and the plain fact is, you *are* different. Not better, not worse—just different! Remember, that difference will become less and less with time. Also remember that you are different in another way. You are probably smarter than most of your so-called normal friends. As you learn to cope with your learning disability, the fact that you are smart will become more and more evident. Chapter 13 on famous learning disabled people offers examples of persons who were thought strange, stupid, or just downright weird but who accomplished much more than all their friends.

CHAPTER 4

Family Responses

F amily responses to diagnosis of a learning disability may range from helpful to disastrous. Some families blame the school system. Others confuse learning disability with mental retardation and either go into mourning or fight back defensively with, "There's nothing wrong with my kid." They may convince the teenager that he is not working hard enough. Some parents may expect less from the teenager, thus giving him or her the message that he should expect less from himself.

Traditionally it has been harder for fathers than for mothers to accept the fact that one of their children is learning disabled. Mothers tend to be more aware of the child's struggles and know how hard he or she has tried.

On the other hand, some parents jump right in and learn as much as possible about learning disabilities. They find out what special help is available and get it for their offspring.

NEGATIVE FAMILY RESPONSES

Some parents respond by becoming upset and defensive. One reaction is to blame the school.

"It's the School's Fault!"

John was having trouble with math. His parents said the teachers were not helping him enough. "You are smart, John; I know you could learn it if they would spend the time to explain it to you. You just don't understand it." John agreed with his parents and became very bitter about his teachers. "The teachers don't like me; they won't help me with my work." John was so convinced of this that he didn't even ask for help. When he finally did, it was at a time when the teacher was very busy. Instead of asking when she would have time, he left feeling rejected. Inside John knew that he wasn't being fair to the teacher, but it was easier just to agree with his dad.

One day his teacher came over and asked if she could help him. Realizing that he didn't have an excuse any more, he said yes. She asked him to come in after school when she could spend more time with him. While they were working, he began talking with her. Before long he was telling her how wrong he had been and about the problem he was having with his dad. The teacher said that many people felt that way and offered to ask the special education teacher and the psychometrist to meet with his father again. John felt better after that. He found that the teacher had become a good friend.

A second negative response to finding out that an adolescent has a learning disability is confusing the diagnosis with mental retardation.

"Oh, No! My Kid's Retarded"

Jim's parents came home very sad from a meeting with school officials. Jim overheard them talking about it: "He's just like my Uncle Elmer. Uncle Elmer wasn't very smart. He quit school in the eighth grade. He just sat around the house till his folks kicked him out. Don't remember what happened to him. Guess I better ask Mom what happened, now that we've got the same problem with Jim. Guess he'll never amount to anything. What will we do with a retarded kid?" Jim ran to his room, slammed the door, and sobbed until his whole pillow was wet with tears. When his mother called him for dinner, he told her he was sick.

Jim didn't sleep that night. His sister came to his room the next morning and said "Jimmy, I couldn't sleep last night. I kept worrying about you. Did you hear what Mom and Dad were talking about in the kitchen?" Jim said he had. His sister told him that she knew he was a lot smarter than she was, and she made straight As. She told him he should go to the school counselor and talk to her about what their folks had said. His sister's support really made a difference to Jim.

A third negative response by parents is to blame themselves for the learning disability.

"This Proves I'm a Failure as a Parent"

June's mother was divorced and was raising two children, June and her younger brother, who was ten. Driving home from school, June's mother blamed herself for not having spent enough time with June. She had to work two jobs to make enough money to live. She started to cry, telling June, "It's all my fault." June felt terrible, partly because she was making bad grades and partly because her mother was so upset. The next day at school she couldn't even concentrate on what the teacher was saying. Her friend Samantha noticed her distress and coaxed the truth out of her. Samantha said that her mother used to feel the same way. June was surprised to learn that Samantha's brother was in special education. Samantha's mother talked to June and invited her and her mother to dinner the next evening. The two mothers had a long talk. When they got home that evening, June's mother gave her a hug, and they both started crying. Now her mother is helping June cope with being learning disabled.

A fourth parental response to learning that an offspring has a learning disability is to try to defend him or her against a perceived attack by the school system.

"There's Nothing Wrong with My Kid!"

Tom's dad shouted at the teacher. At home he yelled at Tom and told him to straighten up and quit acting that way. He said that everyone in their family had been doctors or lawyers and that Tom was going to be a doctor or lawyer too. He said he was going to beat some sense into him, he was going to start whipping him every day he came home with a bad grade. Tom stood there as long as he could with his dad yelling at him. Everything was just a blur. He went into the bathroom and began throwing up.

Tom did not know what to do next. Try as hard as he could, he could not make his grades any better. He went to the special education teacher and told her what his father had said and threatened to do. The teacher promised to talk to his mother and father together. She said lots of fathers felt that way at first. "Don't make the same mistake he's making with you. Be patient with him. He'll come around after I talk to him." Luckily his father did "come around." Some of them don't.

Sometimes the siblings of a teenager with a learning disability respond to such an assessment by becoming self-conscious or embarrassed and try to hide the fact from their friends.

"Don't Tell My Friends"

Sue's sister told her never to tell anyone. "Sue, I would be so embarrassed if my friends knew. No one would understand about your problem. It's better if we never tell anyone. We'd better not even tell Sally because she might tell. Besides, she wouldn't understand about your problem."

Sue felt as if she had a contagious disease. She felt dirty all over. In fact, she went to the bathroom and took a shower, but somehow it didn't help. Finally Sue told her mother what her sister had said. Her mother got right to the root of the problem by assigning a research paper for her sister to do. The topic? "Using positive reinforcement to overcome learning disabilities."

Other family members attempt to protect the diagnosed teenager from the world.

"You Poor Baby, I'll Protect You!"

Johnny's mother said, "That's all right, honey, I'll buy you a banana split, and that will make everything seem better.

When you get up in the morning, everything will be all right. We'll show that teacher she is wrong. If she says anything else to you, you just come and tell me. I'll tell her a thing or two!" She made a point of cooking all his favorite foods. When Johnny started gaining weight and his friends began teasing him, Johnny decided he had better grow up and tell his mother to bug off. He went to the school counselor and told him he needed to talk. "Mom's driving me crazy," he began . . .

Sometimes family members respond by blaming the person who has been assessed as learning disabled.

"I Always Knew You Were Stupid"

"Man, are you stupid! You really did it to the family this time. Why are you like this anyway? I don't even want to live in the same house as you." Bart went out, slamming the door. He started walking. He didn't even realize where he was until he almost bumped into Julie. Julie was in his class; in fact, she went to special education class. Julie was really pretty. No one treated her differently. Julie asked him what was wrong. Bart said, "I got problems with my brother." He started walking on again. Julie said, "Mind if I walk with you, Bart? I'm going to the grocery store to get some things." Bart said, "Oh, guess not." As they walked along, he found that Julie was really easy to talk to. Before he knew it he was telling her all about his brother's reaction. She was very understanding, having been through the same thing. Somehow just talking to someone who understood made things better. In fact, Julie and Bart both felt better. It was going to be kind of nice being in the same special education class as Julie.

POSITIVE FAMILY RESPONSES

Basically, negative family responses to finding out that a teenager has a learning disability tend to discourage the teenager and cripple his or her ability to cope with the problem. On the other hand, positive responses tend to encourage the teenager and enable him or her to respond to the information in creative ways that will ultimately lead to dealing with it successfully.

Some families respond to the diagnosis of learning disability by saying, "We're in this with you. We will learn everything we can about it, and we will do it together." This response greatly encourages the diagnosed teenager because his or her parents have united in the face of a crisis.

"Let's Learn About This Together!"

Dominic and his family were early for their appointment with the school counselor. As they waited, Dominic glanced anxiously first at his mother and then at his father. He was very worried. None of this made sense to him. For ten years he had tried to get good grades. Everyone else in the family had always gotten good grades. Despite all of his efforts, Dominic was a C student; sometimes worse. Now the counselor in the new school had given him a whole series of tests. Maybe this would be the answer. As the office door opened, Dad reached over and ruffled his hair good-naturedly. Mom winked at him. Then Mrs. Jones walked into the room with a huge pile of folders in her arms.

"Good afternoon," she said. "Boy, have I got good news for you. We have discovered that Dominic is a very bright person." His father interjected, "That doesn't surprise me at all." "Me either," said his mother. "Well, it really doesn't surprise me either," said the counselor. "That's one reason I wanted Dominic to be tested. He just seemed too smart to be struggling so much." She went on to explain that the tests showed that Dominic had a learning disability. His parents were very much interested in what she had to say. Later they got from the library several books dealing with learning disabilities. Within a matter of weeks they were experts.

In fact, the whole family became experts. Not only did they understand what learning disabilities were, but they knew all about Dominic's disorder—he had a fine motor problem. Soon they were involved in helping him develop strategies to overcome the problem. The result was that Dominic was making As and Bs by the end of the semester.

The most positive response that a family can make to a learning disabled teenager is one of confidence.

"We Believe in You!"

Louise still remembers the sound of her mother's voice when they sat in the principal's office. The psychometrist was explaining the test results, and the special education teacher was explaining what a learning disability is. Her mother spoke up proudly, "I am very proud of Louise. I believe in her. I know that with this information she can turn her life around." Tears come into Louise's eyes every time she thinks of it. Her father was killed in the war, and she and her mother have had a rough time getting by financially. Some weeks they do not have enough money to buy all the groceries they need. The school provides free lunches, and that helps a lot. Her mother works long hours cleaning houses, and the people sometimes give her a meal and give her clothes for Louise that their children no longer need. That helps a lot too. Just knowing that her mother believes in her makes her feel like the richest person in the world.

Teenagers who have just found out that they have a problem with learning need to be able to make a distinction between learning disabilities and outright stupidity. Family members' responses can make all the difference.

"I Know How Smart You Really Are!"

When Mike's parents heard the analysis of the tests, his dad said, "See, now *they* know how smart you are. I knew it all along." His mother reached over and touched his shoulder. The teacher looked pleased and said, "Yes, we all knew how smart Mike was. We just didn't know why his grades were not as high as they should have been. Now he can get some special help and things will be better. He will have to work hard, but he can do it."

It is really helpful to a learning disabled adolescent to discover that one of his or her parents is also learning disabled. If the parent has not mentioned it, the information comes as a welcome surprise. It helps to normalize what may at first seem very abnormal to the teenager.

"I Had That Problem Too!"

William's dad had told him that he had had school problems as a boy. He had been in a learning disability class and had gone to a special college that worked with learning disabled students. His dad had a good job now and made good money. He explained to William that he would have to work harder than the other students. It really helped William to have his dad as an example, showing that he could be successful in life even with a learning disability.

Many parents hold as a primary belief that every person is unique. In such case the teenager already feels special.

"It's Just Another Way You're Special!"

When Carolyn's parents found out that she was learning disabled, they gave her a big hug and said, "You have always been the most beautiful girl in the world to us. We know you're smart. Now we know you are special in other ways too. You are really one of a kind. There will never be another Carolyn just like you." Carolyn felt good about herself when she heard her parents say that. She was ready to tackle the world again with her enthusiastic nature.

Some families have a philosophy that says, "We are winners!" To such a family the knowledge that one of its members is learning disabled really makes no difference.

They never seem to question their winning philosophy, never accept the idea of defeat.

"It May Just Take Longer!"

Tiffany's family had always been winners. They never accepted anything else as possible. Her paternal grandfather had been a war hero, as had her father. While her grandfather was away fighting the war, her grandmother had supported the family by driving a munitions truck. Her maternal grandmother had enlisted in the American Red Cross. There she met her future husband, Tiffany's grandfather, a Red Cross official. Their first child, Tiffany's mother, became their state's first woman member of Congress. Tiffany's father had contracted polio as a child and suffered a crippled right leg. He viewed his disability as nothing more than a slight handicap. It did not stop him from winning a letter in football. So when the school counselor told her parents that Tiffany was learning disabled, they simply said, "Well, maybe it will take you a little longer to become a doctor."

CHAPTER 5

"So That's Why Kids Think I'm Strange"

I n this chapter we shall discuss some reasons why your peers may treat you like someone from another planet. That can be painful, but it doesn't have to ruin your life. You can do something about it, but first you need to be aware of the reasons.

Difficulty Communicating Thoughts

Freddie, a seventh-grader, had difficulty with oral expression. He got so tired of having people look at him strangely when he explained things. They never seemed to understand what he was talking about, and he never understood why. The speech pathologist had been working with him for a year. His mother and teachers said they could see a lot of improvement, but Freddie couldn't. In fact, Freddie had not seen any improvement until yesterday. Yesterday made all that work with the pathologist worth every second. He was talking to Jenny Lynn, and she understood everything he was saying. She gave him a big smile and reached over and touched his arm. WOW! Then she said, "Freddie, I really enjoyed talking with you. Could you come over tonight and help me study for the math test tomorrow? You explain the problems better than the teacher does."

Social Interaction

Many students with learning disabilities are so preoccupied with their problems that they do not relate well to other students.

Suzanne, an eighth-grader, walked down the hall to her next class feeling very lonely and thinking about what her teacher had said in math class. She had been so embarrassed when she could not answer his questions. She was sure all the other kids were laughing and talking about how stupid she was. She walked past Mary, Patsy, and Marie and didn't even see them, let alone speak to them. What Mary, Patsy, and Marie really were saying was, "Has Suzanne ever spoken to you? She has never spoken to me. I guess she doesn't like any of us."

Suzanne also walked past John and Jake. John said, "Suzanne is really pretty, but I'm afraid to ask her for a date. She looks mad all the time, and she never speaks to any of us."

What would have happened if Suzanne had looked them straight in the eye and said a big friendly, "Hi"! as she passed them? You're right. She would probably have been asked for a date.

Different Dress and Hairstyle

Some kids with learning disabilities dress in unusual ways. That may be because things look different to them, but it could also be that they are afraid to get too close to other kids. Being different sometimes makes them feel safe.

Bill, an eighth-grader, had his own way of dressing. He liked certain types of clothes, and he liked to wear his hair longer than the other kids. Bill was in constant conflict with his parents and teachers. His style was very important to him. If people did not like him because of it, he felt they were not to be trusted anyway. They were not the type of people he wanted for friends. According to Bill, they were prejudiced and snobbish and did not understand sensitive people with deep feelings. Bill failed to understand that he was just as prejudiced about them as he thought they were about him. Most people find it hard to relate to people who seem different from them.

Clumsiness

Celia, a ninth-grader, has some gross motor difficulty and tends to bump into things and people. She has spatial difficulties that prevent her from realizing where she is in relation to other objects in space.

Walking into her classroom yesterday, Celia bumped into Azure, a basketball star and one of the most popular students in the school. Celia had been wishing all year that Azure would notice her and speak to her. When she bumped into him, they both dropped all their books. Celia was so embarrassed that she ran down the hall and out of school. She ran all the way home and cried all afternoon.

When her mother came home she found Celia sitting in her bedroom in the dark. Celia's mother talked with her all evening, but nothing helped.

The next morning, Saturday, Celia's mother came into her room and said she had a surprise. She had read in the morning paper that the YWCA was offering a modeling class for teenagers that very day. She had already enrolled Celia by telephone.

When they were ready to go it was pouring rain. Celia didn't want to go, but her mother insisted. At the Y her mother paid the fee and promised to be back at one o'clock to get her. Celia didn't want her to go, but she was afraid to say so in front of all the people.

Because of the rain, only five girls enrolled that day. Celia did not know any of them. The instructor had many good ideas. She showed them how to walk, how to go up and down stairs, how to hold their head, how to speak to people, and many other useful things that no one had ever told Celia before. She made Celia feel like a really special person—a glamorous person.

When Celia's mother came to get her, Celia was excited and happy. She felt good about herself. She practiced the rest of the weekend walking and holding her body in a glamorous position when she walked and talked.

When Monday morning came Celia was not ready to go to school. She told her mother that she was sick. Her mother said she understood but that Celia had to go anyway. Celia dreaded going to the office to get her admit slip. She told the secretary that she had been sick and had to go home on Friday. She was surprised when the secretary handed over her books, saying that Azure had brought them in.

Celia took a deep breath and started down the hall with her new "glamorous" walk. Near the classroom she saw Azure. As she was trying to think of how to apologize to him, he came up and said, "On the basketball court they say I foul when I bump into someone, and I'm penalized. Since I bumped into you, I guess I'll have to buy you a Coke after school." Celia's heartbeat was so loud she was afraid he would hear it. Again she took a deep breath and with her new glamorous voice said, "I would like that." Azure gave her a big grin and said he would meet her at the Quick-Shop at four o'clock.

As Celia started to walk, she wasn't sure her legs would work at all, let alone walk in the new way she had learned. Inside she was ecstatic. This time she had to take two deep breaths before she could take the few steps into the classroom. Later, as she thought back on it, she wasn't sure if she had remembered her glamorous walk or not.

Gangs

Learning disabled kids often get involved with street gangs because gangs give them a temporary feeling of belonging.

Chipper was a ninth-grader. His parents were divorced, and his mother's job required her to work nights. His older brother was a member of a gang. Chipper didn't really want to join; he didn't want to be involved in drugs or stealing. But that was where all the cool kids were.

Chipper didn't feel comfortable with the other kids at school. They thought he was strange and treated him as if there was something wrong with him.

Chipper loved his mother, but she was never home. He

missed her a lot. She had a boyfriend, and when she wasn't working, she was with him. She had told Chipper that she loved him but he would soon be grown and gone, and she had to look out for herself. He understood that—or at least he tried to understand it. He just knew deep down that he loved her and missed her. He had never really gotten to know his father. He knew his dad was not interested in him or he would call sometimes.

Chipper never let anyone know how lonely he was. The gang would take up part of that empty space. He could feel that he really belonged to something. It was scary to feel you didn't belong anywhere and no one cared enough about you to be there when you needed them.

Chipper joined the gang, and after thinking it through he was proud of that decision. The gang would be his family. A family that would stand by him. A family that would be loyal to him. A family that would protect him even if it meant killing for him.

Of course, as in all families, being a member meant doing things he didn't like. He didn't like doing chores, nor did he like stealing or using drugs, but different families require different things. "Oh, well," he thought, "I guess I'll just have to grit my teeth and do it."

Chipper was too young to understand the difference between family loyalty and support and a gang that just talked that way but merely used him. The gang manipulated him to do what they wanted. Chipper was caught breaking into a house and went to jail. It was his mother who came and stood by him, not the gang. His fellow members said they had never heard of him; they said he was stupid for getting caught.

What could Chipper have done to prevent this from

happening? If he had asked for help in communication and social skills, he might have developed friendships with other students that could have given him a sense of belonging. He could have told his mother about his feelings of loneliness. She might have responded differently.

Remember, gang membership is always a one-way street. A one-way relationship is not healthy. There has to be give and take in a healthy relationship. Each has to be truly interested in the welfare of the other. This most often happens in a family, not in a gang.

CHAPTER 6

"What Can I Do?"

"**D**o I just give up? Is there any hope I can be like other kids?" That hopeless feeling can completely overwhelm you if you let it. We never get everything we want in life. We all have to find ways to compensate for what we don't have. In other words, we find ways to get by.

SURVIVAL IS THE NAME OF THE GAME

First you must figure out if you are an *auditory* (you learn best what you hear), a *visual* (you learn best what you see), or a *kinesthetic* (you learn best what you feel) learner. How do you remember a thing best—when you hear it, when you see it, or when you feel it? When people tell you something, do you picture in your mind what is being said, do you just concentrate on the words, or do you actually feel it?

A radio announcer was reporting on a car wreck at the corner of Western and Second streets. One of the authors is a visual learner. While she was picturing the location in her mind, the announcer had already sped through the news. Too late she realized that she had missed the last ten sentences. This is common for visual people when listening to the radio; they find television much more effective. Radio, on the other hand, is great for auditory learners, who really tune in on words.

Melinda

Melinda was a auditory learner. She found it very hard to learn by reading unless someone were reading aloud. Melinda's father liked to watch the news on television during dinner. One evening he had the volume turned up extra loud when Melinda began asking him about his new car. He tried to pay attention to her and the TV, but he simply couldn't do both. He was a visual learner, whereas Melinda was auditory. Before she knew what was happening, her father stood up and shouted, "Why in thunder can't you keep quiet when I'm watching television?"

Melinda had placed him in an almost impossible situation: He simply could not separate out the competing distractions. Auditory learners sometimes get in trouble because they don't realize that other people can't listen to several conversations at once.

A very different picture is presented by the kinesthetic learner, who is more attuned to how an event feels. One of the authors is a kinesthetic learner. He has earned quite a reputation in his field of marriage and family therapy because of his ability to sense what is going on in a family long before the problem is revealed to him. He simply feels what they feel.

As a child he had difficulty because he sensed that other people were angry and wrongly believed that they were angry with him. This can be a big problem for kinesthetic learners.

WHERE DO YOU FIT?

The following is a step-by-step procedure to help you discover and cope with your particular learning style. First, it is important to find out if you are an auditory, a visual, or a kinesthetic learner. Copy the test, and check the blank on each line that most applies to you.

Learning Styles Test

Visual	Auditory	Kinesthetic
— I picture words	— I sound out words	— Spelling is hard
— I say "I see"	— I say "I hear you"	— I say "Feels right"
— I remember what a friend wore	— I remember what a friend said	— I remember if my friend was fun
— I like computers	— I like music	— I like a warm bath
— I like art	— I like history	— I like English Lit
— I'm distracted by bright colors	— I'm distracted by loud noises	— I'm distracted by minor pains
— I enjoy playing video games	— I enjoy listening to the radio	— I enjoy acting
— I am quiet	— I like to talk	— I like sports
— I like to write neatly	— I write legibly	— I write sloppily
— I like to be in style	— Style is not that important	— I like comfortable clothes
— TOTAL	— TOTAL	— TOTAL

Note: Total the checks in each column. The column with the most checks should be your primary learning style.

The second step is to figure out what you need to learn. A person with reading problems has trouble sorting through all those words to decide what is the most important thing to learn. It's not that you can't learn it; you just don't know what "it" is.

You need an old copy of your textbook, perhaps one that has been damaged. Your teacher may be able to help you find one. You also need a highlight pen, one that makes transparent marks; choose yellow, blue, red—your favorite color. Now get your teacher to help you highlight the important things to learn in your current assignment.

Third, use one of the following strategies:

Visual Learners
Look at the words you highlighted, read them, close your eyes and picture them in your mind over and over again. When you are eating breakfast try to picture them with your eyes open. Your ability to visualize is a very powerful tool.

Auditory Learners
Say the highlighted words over and over again. Record them on a tape recorder and play the tape back, listening to yourself. While you are eating breakfast hear your words over and over again. Get a friend or family member to help by reading your assignments to you. Soon you will be able just to say the words aloud and hear them in your mind as if they were on tape. Some people have learned to read the words to themselves and hear them as if they were saying them aloud.

Kinesthetic Learners
You need to convert what you want to learn into feeling-type material to help you remember it. Copy the high-

lighted material from the book onto three-by-five cards. Carry the cards with you and pull them out whenever you have a few minutes. If you are reading about rotten eggs, you can try to recall how awful they smell while you are reading about them. If you are reading about someone's being angry, you know how you would feel if that happened to you. If a girl you are reading about was wearing a velvet dress, in your mind you can feel the softness and smoothness of the velvet.

It is important for kinesthetic learners to make learning fun. A kinesthetic learner might not be able to remember how to spell *acquires*, but he or she could remember "Art couldn't quit using Red Eye's snuff."

All learners need to understand the importance of repetition. Study the material over and over again until you can remember it.

Learning is simply finding out how you learn best and using it to your advantage. You might even try the strategies for all the learning methods: You could be a combination learner.

Test-Taking Skills

Taking tests can often be anxiety-producing for learning disabled teenagers. We suggest that you take the following steps. Try to relax. You will be able to do a better job if you are relaxed.

Go through the questions quickly, reading each one and responding with the first answer that comes to your mind. It is more likely to be correct than answers you think of later. Skip questions that you do not know. When you have finished answering the ones you do know, go back and try to answer the questions you skipped. Then read all the questions again to see if you would like to change any answers. Since most tests have a time limit, this technique allows you to answer more questions.

If you are an auditory learner, remember to hear the questions as you read them, then hear the answers as you write them. If you are a visual learner, remember to visualize your answers before you write them. If you are a kinesthetic learner, remember to go inside yourself to find out if the answers feel right.

Practice

There are many exercises geared toward helping people with learning disabilities. These exercises may seem repetitive and boring, but they have been proved to help. For example, a special education teacher may ask a person with reading difficulties to do dozens of repetitions of an exercise like this:

Say the word "ball." Is the word "ball" hidden in:
Ballgame?
Baseball?
Cowboy?
Bolt?

Or this one:

Say "slip." Now say "lip."
Say "spoon." Now say "soon."

And this one:

Say "base." Now, instead of "s," use "k," for "bake."
Say "drink." Now, instead of "i," use "a," for "drank."

For people with visualization disorders, therapists use optical teasers and special graphics to help them rewire their sense of vision. Many of these exercises can be fun, but you have to work hard at them.

Behavior Modification Program

If you are having trouble making yourself study, try writing your own behavior modification program. Figure out one thing you want to change. Remember, only one at a time. Then set a penalty and a reward for yourself. Suppose you know you need to spend two hours studying each evening and you don't want to. You can force yourself to do it by writing your own behavior modification program.

First decide on a penalty; perhaps no telephone until you have finished your two hours of studying. Next choose a reward. Do you like frozen yogurt?

Last, you need a penalty and a reward for the weekend. The first week the penalty and reward should be for a total of five hours; the second week, for a total of six hours; the third week, for seven hours; the fourth week, for eight hours; the fifth week, for nine hours; and the sixth week, for ten hours.

If you were not able to reach your weekly study goal, the penalty might be denial of a fun event. You also need to choose a weekend reward if you succeed in reaching your study goal. Perhaps you might buy yourself an album you have been wanting.

Make a copy of this chart to record your behavior modification program. It is crucial to the success of the program that you start with a smaller goal and increase the hours each week.

Behavior Modification Chart

	Time Spent Studying	Reward	Penalty
Monday			
Tuesday			
Wednesday			
Thursday			
Friday			
Weekend			

This activity helps you learn your own inner structure, which is the ultimate in maturity. Many people have become adults without ever learning to have an inner structure; consequently they can never be regarded as truly mature no matter what their age.

Humor as a Coping Technique

Without humor it is difficult for anyone to survive—learning disabled or not. Think of the really happy people you know, people who are fun to be around. They have the ability to laugh both at things that happen and at themselves. Research has shown that the ability to laugh can help us feel better and live longer.

Stress can aggravate learning disorder symptoms. When we are under stress, we can't remember what we really know. In fact, current research shows that tension can be alleviated by the ability to find humor in situations.

Humor can also be used as a coping technique when someone irritates you. Suppose the school bully has a way of picking on you. A visual person can imagine pouring a pitcher of cold water over the bully's head and watching him sputter. An auditory person can imagine the bully's words garbled as if he were talking underwater. A kinesthetic person can pretend the bully feels a winter blast of snow that makes him shiver.

In addition to a good sense of humor, there are several other valuable assets one can have. Following are such assets and related case studies.

Develop a positive attitude.   With a positive attitude you can learn to overcome many difficulties. Remember that the more positive you are, the more positive other people will be toward you.

Marcie

Marcie had several learning disabilities—a developmental arithmetic disorder, an expressive disorder, dyslexia, and a discrimination disorder. In fact, Marcie was the most severely learning disabled person anyone at her school had ever known. The school psychologist who evaluated her couldn't even give her a reading score: she couldn't read a single word. Nevertheless, almost from the beginning Marcie's enthusiastic spirit showed through. She was absolutely determined to overcome her problems. She studied daily and persuaded her parents to hire a math tutor to help her twice a week.

She got the names of dyslexia specialists. Then she phoned them and questioned them thoroughly about their backgrounds, credentials, and success records in treating dyslexia. She arranged with a church for volunteers to drive her to and from treatment. After deciding which specialist she wanted to treat her, she told her parents about him. They were astonished that she had done so much on her own.

Her special education teacher was also impressed with her. Every day Marcie came bounding into the classroom saying, "What are we going to work on today?" Her progress was surprising. Within a remarkably short time, Marcie was able to read a sixth-grade book. The teacher said that she had caught up several of the years that she had been behind.

Believe in yourself. Remember the childhood story, "The Little Engine That Could"? The mother of one of the authors read that story to him over and over. She always ended by saying, "You can do anything that you truly believe you can do." Most people believe that having faith is important. Perhaps one of the most important aspects of faith is belief in yourself. Teenagers who believe in themselves are far better equipped to deal with life, including learning disabilities.

Alyn

Alyn grew up in a family of high achievers. His older sister had graduated from Harvard, and his older brother was a sophomore at Yale. From the very beginning, Alyn had trouble matching their high school records because he had a developmental reading disorder. At first it had seemed to his teacher and his parents that Alyn was not as bright as his siblings, but the test results showed something quite different. His IQ of 142 was actually ten points higher than his sister's and fifteen higher than his brother's. The school psychologist said that Alyn was two grades behind in reading, but that because of his high intelligence level and his belief in himself he had probably already overcome as much as three grade levels.

Don't give up your dream. Everyone has a dream, a life goal, something they want more than anything else in the world. If you can keep your eye on your dream you very likely will accomplish it. Remember Martin Luther King's famous speech, "I Have a Dream." Many people thought that his dream was an impossibility; in fact, many were violently opposed to it. But Dr. King did not forget his dream, and now even after his death much of it has come true. It is possible that your dream will come true as well.

Melanie

Melanie wanted to be a Hollywood actress. She wanted it more than anything in the world. She read everything about acting and about Hollywood. She read scripts aloud, even though they sounded weird because of her articulation disorder. Throughout her years in speech therapy Melanie fantasized about being an actress. When her speech pathologist gave her assignments she pretended that she was playing a starring role as a teenager with an articulation problem. In her mind's eye, she imagined herself sitting with her friends at the Academy Awards ceremony hearing the speaker say, "And the award for Best Actress goes to Melanie for her astounding portrayal of a learning disabled teenager." Even though Melanie never actually became a Hollywood actress, she did overcome her articulation problems—and she did achieve fame in a high school play that she herself wrote, starring Melanie as Helen Keller.

Be the best you can be. Not everyone can be a star, but everyone can be his or her best. You may not be able to be the quarterback of the football team, but you could be a very good sports writer. What is important is striving for excellence, not actually achieving it.

Jacob

Jacob's father was a science professor. He wanted his son to follow in his footsteps. The problem was that Jacob absolutely hated science. Jacob had a sequencing disorder, and whenever he tried to do a scientific experiment he got the steps in the wrong order, which was very frustrating. But he loved working on old cars. By the time he was fourteen he was one of the best mechanics in town. His father continued to pressure Jacob to become a scientist. Finally, Jacob confronted him, saying, "Dad, I'm never going to be a scientist! I love being a mechanic. I know that will disappoint you, but I'd like your support. I need your love, but being a scientist is just not for me." His father looked sternly at him for a moment, then began to smile. Tears welling up in his eyes, he said, "I love you, son. Be the best mechanic you can be." And he was.

CHAPTER 7

Special Education

I n special education you receive an *individualized educational program* (IEP). Your special education teacher, a psychometrist (the person who gave you the tests), your school principal, and your parents write your IEP. You need to read it carefully and be sure you are getting what you need. If not, ask to have it changed. All IEPs can be changed at any time if the team agrees. By law the team has to meet at least once a year to discuss your IEP. You will be retested every three years to see if you continue to qualify for special education.

The IEP states what the teacher will do to help you and what she expects of you. It states at what level you are working in the area in which you need help. If you are reading at fourth-grade level now, the teacher may expect you to be reading at sixth-grade level by the end of the year. She will outline what she will do to help you reach that goal. It will take hard work on your part. Sometimes parents are also asked to help. They might be asked to help you with homework or to listen to you read.

Your Parents' Rights

You will be given a copy of your rights when you sign the IEP. They are printed on the back of most forms. The most important thing to remember is that both the school and you are committed to following the IEP.

Your parents can take anyone they wish to the meeting, which will include at least four people from the school. You as a teenager can ask to attend the meeting. Many authorities recommend that teenagers do attend. People usually work harder when they are part of the original planning.

You can request equipment, such as a tape recorder for an auditory learner. If the equipment will increase learning, the school is required to provide it, but be sure it is specified on the IEP. If you need a private work area to prevent distraction, the school can provide that also—but be certain it is something you really want. If you worry that the other students will make fun of you, rethink it. You may feel too uneasy separated from them to be able to concentrate. Request in your IEP that your classroom teacher allow you to go to the special education classroom during study time.

If you have any health problem that interferes with your learning, have your doctor write a letter explaining it to the school.

Shannon

Shannon was a high school student whose reading and math scores were well below her level. She thought she was stupid. Her teachers thought she was lazy, and her parents thought she needed motivation. In fact, Shannon had average to above-average intelligence. However, her ability to learn was hindered by the combined effects of severe dyslexia and attention-deficit disorder.

Shannon's parents were familiar with dyslexia. Her older brother received special tutoring for it from a young age. His disability was easy to diagnose because it was accompanied by hyperactivity. Shannon, who was not hyperactive, hid the fact that she couldn't read and was labeled by her high school as a slow learner who needed more motivation. Her parents applied pressure for her to try harder.

At school, Shannon was struggling, but she was afraid to ask for help. She was afraid of what the teachers would think if they found out she was dumb. When she desperately altered a report card in ninth grade, Shannon's mother requested that the school perform an evaluation. This time the school's psychologist recognized her dyslexia.

The school system first proposed that Shannon be placed in a small class of mentally retarded and emotionally disturbed students. Her parents wanted her to get help that was more geared toward her specific disability. The school system then generated an IEP that would supplement her regular classroom routine.

The plan fell short of Shannon's parents' expectations. Under the plan, Shannon's goal at the end of the ninth grade was to be reading at a fifth-grade level. Shannon's parents then suggested that she be placed in an adjacent public school. The school system refused. Shannon was removed from her public school by her exasperated parents and enrolled in a private academy that specialized in learning-disabled children. By the time she graduated, Shannon was reading at grade level. She went on to a technical school to study physical and occupational therapy.

Angry with the school system, Shannon's parents invoked the federal Americans with Disabilities Act in a court suit seeking reimbursement for the cost of Shannon's private schooling. The law states that students with disabilities are entitled to "free appropriate public education." The courts ruled in favor of Shannon's parents, emphasizing that parents are entitled to reimbursement of private costs if the public school system does not offer appropriate special education.

Role of the Regular Classroom Teacher

A critical item to put in the IEP is that the *regular* teacher make modifications for maximum learning. Regular teachers usually do modify their standard curriculum, so that is omitted from most IEPs, but it should never be eliminated. Examples of such modifications are the following:

1. A student with fine motor difficulties may take tests by answering questions verbally instead of in writing.
2. A student with fine motor difficulties may be supplied with prewritten math problems and may just enter the answers.
3. Certain students may take tests orally by having the teacher read the questions aloud.

If the school is not willing to cooperate, your state has a child advocacy group that will assist you. Most schools are eager to do whatever they can to help you learn best.

Meshell

Meshell's mother asked her brother-in-law to attend the IEP meeting. Meshell's uncle had placed three of his children in special education and had been to many meetings. He talked with Meshell before the meeting. Meshell had a reading problem. She was a visual learner and learned best if she could see the information. Her science teacher taught by lecturing. During the IEP meeting, it was arranged that the science teacher would write information on the board when he explained it to the class. In that way Meshell could see what he talked about. It was also requested that tests be given on her reading level.

Juan

Juan's mother, a single parent, was having trouble with him. He was so angry about not being able to read that he yelled at her and was always fighting with his brothers and sisters. He would not let her help him at all. At the meeting, Juan's mother cried and asked for help both in dealing with Juan and with his reading problem. Because the home situation was interfering with Juan's reading, the IEP was written to cover private counseling for both him and his mother.

William

William, thirteen, had an auditory figureground disorder. He heard all the sounds around him at the same time: the birds outside, the teacher talking in the room next door, and the telephone ringing across the hall. No wonder he could not understand what his teacher was saying. His doctor came to the IEP meeting to explain what was happening to William. He requested that the school provide special earplugs for William to wear when he needed to work quietly at his desk. Because William was embarrassed to wear the earplugs in front of his friends, he was allowed to study in the special education room. This was all written in the IEP. William's grades improved after he had a quiet place to study.

Dusty

Dusty, thirteen, and his father lived alone. His dad could not get off work to attend the IEP meeting, so the school team agreed to meet with him at 7:30 a.m. Most schools are glad to work with parents. They are interested in you and want to help you.

CHAPTER 8

Dealing with Classroom Teachers

S ome teachers are either thoughtless or cruel. They make hurtful remarks such as, "Methuselah was slow, but he was old." "How many times do I have to tell you that?" "Don't you ever listen?" Other teachers will do anything in their power to help you. The key to getting all kinds of teachers to help you is a sincere and willing attitude. This should be combined with some- times ignoring their comments and sometimes explaining your position in an assertive manner. Assertiveness re- quires that you never place blame. Instead, you express your feelings calmly. You are not responsible for another's actions, only your own.

Teachers and schools have rules that you, your friends, and perhaps your parents may think are stupid. Rules are like taxes. No one likes paying taxes, but our country runs on the system of taxation. The schools run on a system of rules. We have to learn to follow all kinds of rules in life.

The sincere and willing attitude mentioned above involves four steps:

1. Asking for help.
2. Organizing a plan.
3. Putting the plan into action.
4. Reporting your progress to the teacher daily or weekly.

Be sure to report what works and what does not work. That will enable your teacher to help you adjust to the program. Sometimes the program may need to be changed. Don't skip any of the steps; each one is important in working with your teacher.

June

June's teacher, Mrs. Jaye, had arthritis. It was very painful for her to drag herself to school. By the time she got to her classroom, she was exhausted and had to rest for a while.

As her first-hour class arrived, Mrs. Jaye was still in pain. When the bell rang and the students sat down, she pointed to instructions on the chalkboard to do page 51 in their English workbooks.

June didn't see the teacher motion to the chalkboard. Without thinking she said, "What page?" Mrs. Jaye barked at her, "If you can't read, you should be in the stupid class." June was so embarrassed that she almost cried. She could read well, but she did have dyscalculia and was in a learning disability class for math. She was very sensitive about being called stupid, so she just sat there holding back the tears.

Mrs. Jaye looked at her again and said, "Are you deaf,

too?" At that point June managed to get her book out and turn to the correct page. Then she just stared through her tears at the blur of words. She was thinking about what all the other students must be thinking of her. When the bell finally rang she stumbled out of the room, not speaking to anyone. She didn't even know the homework assignment. She just knew that Mrs. Jaye didn't like her, and she couldn't figure out why.

As she walked down the hall Mrs. Nixon, the counselor, stopped her and said, "June, whatever is the matter? You look as if you've lost your best friend." June couldn't hold back any longer. She burst into tears. Mrs. Nixon took her into the office and shut the door, and June poured out what had happened.

After she had calmed down, Mrs. Nixon explained about Mrs. Jaye's health problem and said she would talk to her. She stressed that it was important that June talk to Mrs. Jaye after school. They worked on things she could say to Mrs. Jaye.

After school June took a deep breath and went to the English classroom to talk to Mrs. Jaye, who was busily grading papers. June stood patiently beside the desk. Finally Mrs. Jaye looked up and barked, "What is it you want?" June took a deep breath and said, "Mrs. Jaye, it is very important to me to make good grades in English. I apologize for not paying attention this morning. When you corrected me, I was so embarrassed that I couldn't work the rest of the period. I even missed getting tomorrow's assignment. I was afraid to ask what it was. I will try very hard to pay attention tomorrow. If I do miss something or don't understand something, is there some way you could help me without embarrassing me?" Mrs. Jaye said, "Mrs. Nixon talked to me about you."

June said, "Yes, I talked to Mrs. Nixon. She told me

about your arthritis. I know it must hurt a lot. I broke my arm once and it hurt a lot. Is there anything I can do to help you?" June could hardly believe it when she saw a tear appear in Mrs. Jaye's eye. Without thinking she reached over and gave her a hug. From that time on June and Mrs. Jaye worked very well together and became the best of friends.

Mrs. Jaye also changed her attitude to the other students and became more sensitive to their feelings. She had been so focused on her own pain that she failed to realize how they were reacting to her.

Did you notice how June used a "sincere and willing attitude"? She was assertive in talking to Mrs. Jaye, but she did not say anything critical. She followed the first three steps: she asked for help, she organized a plan, and she put the plan into action. Now she needs to report her progress to Mrs. Jaye.

Rico

Rico was sitting alone in the big room waiting for the hearing officer, the school administrator, the principal, his classroom teacher, his foster mother, and whoever else was coming. It was a very scary place for a fourteen-year-old.

Rico had been through tough times before. Being taken away from his mother last year was hard. His foster mother was nice to him, but she wasn't his mother. He had been mad at everybody since then. His mother wasn't perfect. Maybe she didn't come home for days at a time, and he didn't always have enough to eat, but he knew she loved him.

Rico had never known his father. He had to be the man of the house. Several men had lived with them, but he paid no attention to them. He knew they wouldn't be around long. He was the one his mother really loved. He just wished she would show it more.

Rico looked up and saw all the people coming into the room. The hearing officer sat at the end of the long table and motioned for Rico to sit at his right side. "Rico, I am going to ask your teacher and principal to tell what happened. Then I will ask you to tell your side. Is that fair?" Rico responded, "Yes, sir."

His teacher, Mr. Sampson, said, "Rico threatened to kill me. I had cafeteria duty that day, and Rico was cutting in front of the other students and pushing them around. I yelled across the room at him to straighten up. He didn't pay attention to me, so I went over, took him by the arm, and put him in line. At that point he said he was going to kill me."

The hearing officer turned to the principal and said, "Do you have anything to add?" The principal said, "No, that is the same story both Mr. Sampson and Rico told me."

The hearing officer turned to Rico and said, "Let's hear your side." Rico said, "That's what happened." The hearing officer said, "Son, you have a right to tell your side." Rico said, "There is nothing else to tell." The hearing officer pressed him, "Why did you say you were going to kill him?" Rico said, "He didn't have any right yelling at me or shoving me around in front of everyone. Nobody's gonna treat me that way!"

The hearing officer gave a deep sigh and said, "Son, we can't go around threatening to kill everyone who displeases us. That attitude can get you in a lot of trouble. You need to get your temper under control. In fact, we can't even allow you back in school until you learn how to control your temper."

The hearing officer turned to the foster mother and asked, "Are you taking Rico for counseling?" She said, "No, Rico has refused to go. He has given me a hard time too."

The hearing officer looked at Rico again and said, "Son, you have a certain amount of energy within yourself to use every day. You can use it arguing with your teacher, your foster mother, and those around you, or you can use it constructively studying and working with them. It is your choice."

Rico knew that he had not been nice to his foster mother. He knew it wasn't her fault the way things were. He also knew he needed help. He was making a mess of things. He was being kicked out of school. What if his foster mother kicked him out too?

The hearing officer looked Rico straight in the eyes and said, "Rico, look at me. This is an extremely serious situation. Are you ready to get help and change your attitude—or do you want me to turn you over to the police?"

Rico didn't like to be threatened, but he knew the hearing officer was right. He said, "Yes sir, I will get help."

CHAPTER 9

Help Beyond
the School

Sometimes learning disabled teenagers need help that the school cannot provide. The school may not have teachers on staff who are trained to deal with your particular learning disability. It could also be that your disability is more severe than the school is equipped to handle. You might need to seek help outside the school because you have become depressed as a result of your disability. Family problems might make it harder to cope with being learning disabled. Or it might be necessary to seek outside help if you are having trouble with a teacher or the principal.

It can be scary trying to find a professional counselor to help with these kinds of problems. Scary, and also very confusing. When you look in the phone directory you find all kinds of counselors: psychiatrists, psychologists, child psychologists, social workers, marriage and family therapists, licensed professional counselors, drug and alcohol counselors. If that list isn't enough to discourage you, nothing will! So where do you start?

Perhaps the best place to start is with your school counselor. Tell him or her what you think the problem is and ask for help in deciding which professional to choose. You must have your parents' permission to do this. Follow your counselor's advice. The following are descriptions of types of therapists that might be helpful.

Marriage and Family Therapists

These professionals are trained to deal with relationship problems. Ask yourself this question: "Is the primary problem between myself and someone else?" If the answer is yes, a marriage and family therapist is exactly what you need. It makes no difference whether the problem is between you and a teacher, you and your boyfriend or girlfriend, you and a brother or sister, or you and your parents. The point is that the problem is a relationship difficulty, and marriage and family therapists are trained to deal with relationships.

Cody

Cody was having a terrible time at home. Ever since he was diagnosed as having a learning disability, life had been miserable. His father thought that Cody just wasn't working hard enough. Every day after school Cody hurried home and started on his homework, hoping to finish it before his father got home. But every evening the same thing happened. Cody would be only half finished when his father hit the door. "Why in thunder aren't you through?" he would bellow. Then would come the lecture: "No kid of mine is going to get away with being lazy. Why, when I was your age I had to work in the fields. I didn't get to sit around and watch TV all night. Learning disability, my foot!" On and on it would go. Cody knew the routine by heart. His father would still be at it when his mother got home. Then she would start screaming. "George, let the boy study. Can't you see that he can't help it? The poor baby is very disturbed. Can't you remember what his teacher said? He has some kind of a learning disturbance. What he really needs is some of Mommy's loving and a good meal."

With that the real fight would start—the one between his mother and father. Sometimes it would go on for hours. Cody thought neither of them would ever understand. He didn't need to be babied by his mother, nor screamed at by his father. It was getting so that he felt absolutely hopeless. His grades were worse now than before they found out about the learning disability. He was so angry that he was beginning to be destructive. His teacher had tried to talk to him about his behavior several times. The final straw was when Cody picked up a desk and slammed it to the floor, breaking it. In desperation, Cody went to his school counselor. There, crying hysterically, he sobbed out the whole story. Much to his surprise, the counselor called in both his father and mother and referred them to a marriage and family therapist.

The therapist listened to all three of their stories. Then he got to the heart of the matter: "Any time you have a teenager out of control, it is because you have two parents who can't agree on parenting strategy." This astonished Cody and his parents. "You mean you think that Cody's problems are our fault?" yelled his father. The therapist said, "It's not your fault that Cody is learning disabled. It *is* your fault that Cody is unable to deal with it better.

Your job is to help Cody, not to punish him or baby him. In fact, the two most damaging parenting styles are the ones that seem opposites of each other: being over-strict or overprotective. Both tell teenagers that they are incompetent."

The therapist spent several sessions teaching Cody's parents how to be better parents. As a result, his father, an engineer, was able to give Cody valuable help with his math. His mother, who had never been a very good student herself, cooked a really nice meal every night as a reward for Cody and his father. Cody could hardly believe the difference. This was the kind of family he had always wanted.

Mental Health Counselors

These professionals deal with emotional problems such as depression and anxiety. They are also very good at help-ing people make decisions and bring order into their lives.

Mendy

Mendy's life was one of absolute confusion. Her grand-father wanted her to be an attorney. Her grandmother wanted her to be a doctor. Her mother thought she would make a great actress, but her father wanted her to take over his import business. Her physical education teacher, who was also the volleyball coach, wanted her on the volleyball team. Her classroom teacher wanted her to spend as much time as possible on her regular studies. Her special education teacher wanted her in special classes for math, reading, and spelling, which would amount to half a day. Mendy's problem was that she tried to make everybody happy and felt guilty when she didn't. As a result she was anxious or depressed most of the time.

Mendy's school counselor was one of the best, but she didn't have time to help Mendy. As the only counselor for 1,600 students, she could deal only with the most severe problems. She referred Mendy to a mental health counselor.

During the next several months the counselor helped Mendy work on her self-image, which was so bad that Mendy later described it as "lower than a centipede with fallen arches." As her self-image improved she began to make decisions based on her needs, not other people's. She decided that she wanted to be a professional dancer. She applied for, and received, a grant to study dance at a major university after graduation from high school. That bothered her parents and her grandparents, but it didn't bother Mendy. She was truly happy about her decision. She also asked her special education teacher to let her focus on reading and spelling; that allowed her to spend more time in her regular classroom. Because she was having a hard time with math, she asked her parents to hire a tutor, which they did. In short, with the help of the mental health counselor, Mendy began taking charge of her life. As she did, her anxiety and depression evaporated. She was laughing for the first time in years and looking forward to her future.

Learning Disability Specialists

These professionals concern themselves specifically with people who have trouble learning.

Albert

Albert had three learning disabilities—an expressive problem so bad that he could hardly say an entire sentence, a discrimination disorder involving both auditory and visual problems, and color blindness. All of these problems can be dealt with, but they take a long time. In Albert's school the special education department had only two teachers for 600 students. Both of them were frank with Albert's parents. They said they didn't have the time, resources, or energy to help him. They suggested a local nonprofit family institute that had a fine clinic for learning disabled children and youth.

Albert's parents visited the institute and were surprised by several things. First, six special education teachers and developmental psychologists were on staff, and highly specialized equipment was available. The head of the clinic for learning disabled children was a nationally recognized author and researcher.

Right away it was discovered that although Albert had severe difficulties with auditory and visual learning, he was very sensitive to feeling. After evaluation the counselor began to teach him using a special set of letters in which the vowels were pink and fuzzy and the consonants were white and smooth. Albert was asked to handle each of the letters, feel them, and name them. Little by little, he began to associate vowels with being soft and fuzzy and pink and consonants with being smooth and hard and white. In that way he learned that consonants and vowels were different and that it took both to make a word. It was slow going, but progress was steady. Within a year Albert was ready for his regular classroom and special education classes at school.

*　　　*　　　*

The kind of help that Albert, Mendy, and Cody got can be very expensive. Therefore, an important consideration is how your parents can afford it. Standard health insurance, which your parents may have through their work, may pay. In fact, most health insurance covers marriage and family therapists and mental health counselors. Learning disability specialists are usually not covered.

Clinics

There are several types of clinics that charge fees. The amount varies greatly from clinic to clinic. Some clinics employ a sliding scale. Their fees are based on the family's income, ranging from $2 to $75 per visit. Others have a step scale; they offer only three fees, for lower-income families (about $25 per visit), middle-income families (about $45 per visit), and upper-income families (about $75 per visit). Still others, sometimes called no-scale clinics, charge everyone the full fee of about $75.

Child guidance clinics. Established by city, county, or state mental health departments, they usually serve specific geographical areas (called catchment areas). An important factor is the length of the waiting list. Some child guidance clinics have waiting lists nine months long.

Church- and synagogue-related programs. Churches and synagogues employ counselors who provide help at greatly reduced cost. Some large religious groups have funded agencies to help people who cannot afford treatment. Such groups include Lutheran Social Services, United Methodist Counseling Services, LDS Social Services, Jewish Family Services, and Catholic Charities.

It is important, however, to get information about the policies of the agency you are considering. It may employ a sliding scale, a step scale, or have no scale. This surprises most people, who think that because they are religious agencies, their services are free. It is also important to find out about the waiting list, and particularly whether they have a track record of success in treating your particular learning disability.

Private practice. This is a term used for professionals who own their own clinics. These clinics are usually the most expensive, often charging full fee to all clients. They also tend to be the most available. Because relatively few people can afford to pay full fee, they usually have very short waiting lists. It is important to find out about their track record in treating your particular learning disability. Some private practitioners have just started their professional careers and thus have little experience in treating the various disorders.

Family institute. These agencies are usually found only in large cities. Often they have a skilled staff and several volunteers who work with learning disabled people. The volunteers often are persons who are learning disabled themselves. It is important to check on their qualifications and track record. The fact that an organization is called a family institute is no guarantee that it treats learning disabilities. Usually family institutes have fairly short waiting lists.

Family institutes offer some services that are seldom available in other clinics. One of those is financial assistance. Also, because of their large volunteer staff, family institutes often are able to transport teenagers from school to the institute.

Vocational rehabilitation. Most states have vocational rehabilitation programs, which can be extremely helpful for learning disabled persons. The main thrust of their services tends to be in helping adolescents pursue career opportunities. They provide aptitude testing and often college tuition grants and scholarships.

Drugs and Medication

A drug called Ritalin has been used successfully to treat attention deficit disorder with and without hyperactivity. Thousands of students and working adults are taking the drug and finding it very helpful. Your specialist may recommend it for you. Because your body will develop a tolerance for the drug, it is useful only as a temporary measure and is no substitute for a regime of study and practice. Other widely used medications include Dexedrine and Cylert. These, like Ritalin, are stimulants that excite your nervous system and have the surprising effect of slowing you down and helping you focus your attention. The medications can have some uncomfortable side effects such as weight loss, sleeplessness, and an irregular heartbeat if they are not taken exactly as your specialist says.

Bobby

Bobby is a third grader who loves to play basketball. He is always last to be picked for the teams, however, because he isn't very good. When he gets the ball and drives up-court for a shot, he is so distracted by the shouts and cheers of his playmates that he can't see the basket. His doctor prescribed Ritalin for him, which he takes every morning after breakfast and again in midafternoon. Immediately, his ability on the court improved. Bobby told his doctor that now, when he gets the ball and drives up-court, there is a net there.

CHAPTER 10

Gifted Kids

G ifted kids with learning disabilities are students of unusually high intelligence who have one or more of the problems discussed in Chapters 1 and 2. Their IQ is usually over 130. They are among the most seldom diagnosed of all students with learning disabilities because they are often able to compensate for many of their difficulties. Other people assume that they are average students who work slowly. The students themselves know something is wrong and often think they are stupid. Frequently they are never diagnosed and go through life without understanding their problem. If they are diagnosed, it is often in later years. Emotional problems may develop as a result of not understanding what is happening to them. Daydreaming, doodling, social withdrawal, failure to complete homework, sullenness, and overemphasis on such interests as cars, gangs, and athletics are common difficulties.

Jiminez

Jiminez struggled all through elementary school. His parents and teachers told him he did not work hard enough. Jiminez worked harder, but it didn't help. He felt that no one understood. "They just don't realize that I am really stupid. Maybe if I work even harder they will never guess." By middle school Jiminez was ready to give up; he was getting further and further behind. By eighth grade he was using diversionary tactics to make people notice his bad behavior instead of the fact that he couldn't do the work.

The girls began noticing Jiminez and flirting with him. He also became popular with many of the other boys. He soon realized that he was getting a lot of attention because of his behavior. He was becoming a class leader. Other students were imitating him. It was a good feeling, a feeling of power. Jiminez realized that it was more than ever important to hide how really stupid he was. Otherwise he might lose his friends and his leadership.

Jiminez was getting disciplinary slips every day and was sent home several times a month. His father said he was tired of being called by the school and told Jiminez to clean up his act. Jiminez knew that his dad didn't really care; he had told many funny stories about how he himself had acted in school.

Jiminez' mother would talk with him by the hour, often with tears in her eyes. She said she knew he was smart and that he could become great if he would just try. One day she went to the school and talked to the counselor about her son. The counselor called Jiminez to his office. He said he realized that Jiminez had great leadership ability and asked if he would work with some younger students who were having problems. Jiminez replied that he didn't have time. At that moment the telephone rang. The counselor answered, listened briefly, and then said, "I have the kind of person you describe sitting right here in my office, but I don't know whether he'll do it. You talk to him." He handed the phone to Jiminez. Jiminez could hardly believe his ears when he learned that it was the mayor of the city. The mayor said he was trying to start an "Inner City Program" for students who were having learning difficulties. He wanted a center where students could come after school and get help in studying. He asked Jiminez to come to and discuss the idea. Well, Jiminez could not say no to the mayor. That was when life began to turn around for Jiminez. He was very successful in his new role. He even got his friends to come and help the younger students. He made a difference in a lot of lives.

Two months later Jiminez went to the school counselor and admitted that he needed help himself. After testing it was found that Jiminez was a gifted learning disabled student. The counselor called a multidisciplinary team meeting that included Jiminez' parents. Jiminez was placed in special classes that taught him to cope with his disability. His grades soared, and his interests began to change. He began to have hope for the future. Jiminez enjoys helping people. He is secretly thinking about becoming a doctor and helping people with their health problems.

Jules

Jules did not even know what a learning disability was. He simply was not interested in school. Reading and spelling were stupid. What interested him was repairing watches and clocks. He would sit by the hour working with a watch. He enjoyed taking it apart and studying all the little moving parts. When he knew how everything worked, he would figure out what was wrong.

One day the math teacher kept the class overtime

because his watch was running slow. Jules offered to fix it, and the teacher said, "Sure, why not? Just bring the pieces back when you're through." He didn't mention that he had had the watch in the shop three times and no one could fix it. His comment made Jules wince, but he didn't say anything. It just made him more determined to fix the watch.

Jules did fix the watch. To the surprise of the math teacher, the watch runs perfectly. Every time he looks down at it he is reminded of Jules, his straight F student. What a puzzle! One of these day he must remember to talk to the counselor about Jules.

It was Jules himself who walked into the office of the school psychologist one day and asked for help. Jules was told his learning style and his strengths and ways to help himself. He began working just as hard on himself and his grades as he did on watches and clocks.

Guy

Guy was failing in school. He was just staying until his parents would let him quit. School had always been a struggle. Guy did not know that he was an auditory learner. He made good money working as a waiter after school and on weekends. He worked his way up in the business until he had a job at one of the best restaurants in the city.

One Saturday evening Guy was surprised to see the principal of his school bring in a group of ten people for dinner. Guy wondered if principals were good tippers. The principal was also surprised to see Guy, whom he knew to be a poor student. Guy took their drink orders without paper or pencil, and the principal expected the worst. But when Guy brought the drinks everything was perfect. "Guess we lucked out that time," the principal thought to himself. Next Guy took their dinner orders, still without paper and pencil. He recited a variety of soups, salads, dressings, vegetables, main courses, and methods of cooking. Everyone in the group ordered different things. The principal was a mathematician; he began calculating how many different ways Guy could goof up those orders.

When the soups and salads arrived, everything was served perfectly. The main course arrived, and not one mistake. The food was excellent. The principal's friends commented on his choice of restaurants, on the good service and the outstanding waiter. When the principal proudly admitted that Guy was one of his students, the group chorused that he must be one of his *top* students. The principal only smiled.

On Monday morning he called the school counselor and told him about Guy. They decided to have Guy tested. As you have probably guessed, he was found to be a gifted learning disabled student. With help, Guy learned to turn his auditory skills and abilities into As in the classroom.

Amanda

When Amanda got home the light was blinking on the answering machine. She eagerly pushed the control to see who had called, but she sighed when she heard her teacher's voice. Her teacher was calling her mother as usual to report that Amanda was daydreaming in class and not doing her work. Amanda erased the message as she had so many times in the past. There was no reason to bother her mother. Her mother was a single parent and worked long hours as a waitress. Amanda promised herself, as she had done hundreds of times that she would do better. She did not want to daydream, but she had heard the same lessons so many, many times. This was her second year in eighth grade, and she was taking the same classes. She could mimic all of her teachers' sing-song voices. She kept her friends laughing by the hour imitating Mr. Simpson or Miss Barnett. She knew how they stood, how they used their hands, and all their vocal inflections.

The next day at school the teacher who had made the telephone call stopped her in the hall and said, "Amanda, do you know when you mother will call me? I left a message on her answering machine." Amanda assured her that her mother would call at her first opportunity and then promptly forgot the conversation. She did try harder to pay attention that day, but it was useless. The classes were so boring that she couldn't concentrate for very long.

When she got home the answering machine light was blinking again. When she played it back, she heard the voice of the principal asking her mother to call about an emergency situation with Amanda. After thinking a moment, Amanda erased the message. She did write a note telling her mother to call, but she did not leave the school phone number.

The next day the principal called over the school inter-com for Amanda to come to the office. To her surprise, there was her mother, looking very upset. As the principal and her mother started talking about the messages, the daydreaming, and the mess she was making of her life, Amanda could not hold herself together any longer. She broke down and started crying. Finally all her feelings about being stupid and being bored and needing her mother poured out of her mouth. She looked up, and her mother was crying too. Then her mother was hugging her.

The principal suggested that Amanda be tested to find out what was happening.

The test results showed her to have an IQ of 135 and to be a gifted learning disabled student. She was given special help in the classroom, and the school provided counseling services for both her and her mother. When Amanda graduated from high school she went on to college. Her mother said, "Now, Amanda, you will have many occupations to choose from. You won't have to be a waitress like me unless you choose to."

CHAPTER 11

Help from Parents and Siblings

Parents love you and want the best for you, but sometimes their way of showing it can be difficult for you. If you are having trouble in school they may blame the teacher or they may blame you.

It is easy to agree when they say it is your teacher's fault. Sometimes teachers do make the problem worse, but the solution is still within you. You are the one who has to find a way to get things back in focus and working.

Communication is the key to leveling with your parents without becoming upset or upsetting them. Communication means telling your parents what is happening and how you feel about it without being critical of them. Only constructive comments are effective in true communication. As lawyers say, "Present your side of the case." Ask your parents to help you or suggest ways to get help. In some situations parents can help. In other situations they confuse the issue. They may be too close to the situation and overreact.

Ernest

Ernest slammed the door and went directly to his bedroom. He had not spoken to his parents for ten days. At mealtimes someone, he guessed it was his mother, knocked on his door and left a tray of food there. Sometimes the food was cold. When he had finished eating he put the tray back outside, and mysteriously it disappeared. Ernest at first had been very angry at his parents. Now he was lonely. He didn't like living this way, but he certainly would never admit it to his parents. They had no business treating him that way. One thing was certain, he would never treat his kids that way. He would always listen to them and support them when they had a problem.

He sat down on his bed and looked at the stack of books in his hands. Being grounded was the pits. Just going to school, walking home, studying, and going to bed—he had been doing it for days. Last weekend he had spent the whole time in his room. Only his Nintendo game had helped him through it.

While he was at school on Monday the Nintendo game had disappeared. In its place was a note in his father's handwriting: "Studying pays better dividends." Ernest's dad was a stockbroker. This was no way for a sixteen-year-old to exist. His TV, his telephone, his car had been taken away; now his Nintendo. He looked at the clock, hardly believing how long he had been sitting there feeling sorry for himself. He thought bitterly, "It's surprising I still have a clock." Getting his books out, he started studying.

Before long he heard sirens approaching. The sound got

louder and louder and finally stopped close by. Next he heard voices downstairs. Opening the door, he saw ambulance attendants carrying someone out of the house on a stretcher. Ernest ran down to where another attendant was talking to his mother, who was sobbing. She turned to him, crying, "Your dad has had a heart attack." The attendant said, "Can you drive your mother to the hospital?" Ernest reached into his pocket for his keys, then remembered. His mother told him where to find her keys. When he got to the car she was already inside, just sitting motionless. He backed out of the garage and headed toward the hospital. His dad had had a heart attack once before, when Ernest was only ten. He remembered how scared he had been. His mother had put her arm around him comforting him as they sat in the emergency room. Now it was going to be his turn to comfort his mother. They drove what seemed like hours without saying a word. At the hospital, Ernest let his mother out and went to park the car. When he got to the emergency room his mother was at the desk giving information on his dad. He put his arm around her, and she just seemed to melt into him. They both started crying. A nurse took them into a private waiting room.

After a while he and his mother started talking. She said they had just finished dinner when his father said he had a pain. He went into the bedroom to lie down. When she finished cleaning the kitchen and went to the bedroom she found him unconscious. She called 911 and administered mouth-to-mouth resuscitation until the ambulance arrived. His mother broke off to tell him how much his dad loved him. "You are the pride of his life. You're all he talks about. He can hardly wait until you finish college and go into business with him."

Ernest had dyscalculia. Math was easy for his dad, so

he had never understood how difficult it was for Ernest. Math was the cause of most of their fights. The latest one had erupted when Ernest asserted that he would never be a stockbroker—"Stockbrokers are boring and stupid." He had been furious at his dad and lashed out to hurt him. At the time, he remembered, he had felt glad. Now he just wished he could take it all back.

The doctor came to the waiting room and told them that Ernest's dad would be in intensive care in the coronary unit for a few days. Then the doctor took them to him. Ernest took a deep breath to keep from crying again. His dad reached out and took Ernest's hand. "You don't have to be a stockbroker, son. I love you any way you are." Ernest leaned over and hugged his dad amid tears streaming down his face. He heard himself saying, "I love you too, Dad. More than I can ever tell you or show you." The doctor motioned for the nurse to take his dad on up to the ICU room. Ernest and his mother cried and cried. It was a long night.

During the next week, Ernest and his mother left the hospital only to shower and get clean clothes. As his dad improved, he wanted to talk. He, his wife, and Ernest spent a lot of time talking about Ernest's future. It was a shame that it took a crisis for this family to find the key to communication.

Leamon

Leamon had dyslexia. None of his brothers or sisters had difficulty in school. His mother had never had trouble in school. She found it hard to accept Leamon's problem. His father had dropped out of school in the 10th grade. He had blamed his teachers for not liking him and not helping him, and he told Leamon that all teachers were mean and hateful. Leamon agreed with his dad, but inside he knew better. He knew that several of his teachers really wanted to help him but just didn't know how.

The school counselor called him one day and said Leamon had been referred to him because of an attitude problem. Leamon told the counselor his dad's opinions about how mean teachers were, and the counselor said, "Let's analyze this." As they talked, Leamon realized that the problems were mostly his own fault. The counselor gave him some pointers on how to talk with his parents.

That evening Leamon told his parents that he needed to talk to both of them, and they sat down around the kitchen table. Leamon said, "I had a long talk with Mr. Brown, our counselor, today. You'll both probably get mad at me, but I need to level with you. You know I have dyslexia and have a lot of trouble reading. That is why I am in special education, to get help. I guess I have been so mad about having dyslexia that I have given some of my teachers a pretty bad time. Somehow I forget the things I do that are wrong and just tell you the things my teachers do. I think it is time I grew up and began taking what I deserve. They can't help me otherwise."

To Leamon's surprise, his dad grinned and said, "I kinda think I did that too, son." Leamon's mother said, "Son, I am proud of you for telling us the truth. I guess we owe your teachers an apology. I will come to the school tomorrow, and we can meet with them to see how we can get you on the right track."

The key was Leamon's admitting to his parents that he had been wrong. It opened up a new door for him to get the added support and help he needed.

Getting Siblings to Help

Siblings can help in a number of ways:

1. Have brothers or sisters read material to you.
2. Have them ask you questions to see if you are understanding it and remembering it.
3. Have them explain complicated material. Sometimes hearing it explained a different way makes it easier to understand.
4. Have them help you work out words called acronyms in which each letter stands for the first letter of the thing you have to remember.

Sometimes brothers and sisters are helpful, and sometimes they are not. They can be supportive, and they can be cruel. They know us well enough to help us get over the worst obstacle or destroy us. What makes the difference? How do you help your brother or sister? What makes you want to help? What makes you say hateful things? I think you have the answer tightly tucked away inside.

We get angry at people who are hateful to us. When they say something mean to us, we either say or think mean things about them. In other words, we give back what we get. Right? Now, let's turn that around. Let's say what we *give* to them we will get back! If we have a bad relationship it may take a while to change it back to a good relationship. No one will trust us until we prove ourselves over and over. The only approach that works is sincerity and honesty in a nonblaming approach. We have to level with them and trust them enough to tell them our feelings. That is hard to do. It takes maturity. How mature are you?

Priscilla

Priscilla was in special education for a learning disability in math. Her parents had ruled that she could not receive telephone calls or see anyone until she finished her homework. Priscilla expected her boyfriend to call sometime that evening, and she had three pages of math to do. She hurriedly began working on it. She finished the first page with ease, but halfway through the second page she got stuck. She knew that her parents would not be home until late. She thought about hiding the homework and telling her mother she had finished it, but she knew that would not work. Her mother was proud of Priscilla's work and her good grades in special education, and she always looked at her homework.

At that moment Priscilla heard her brother's car in the driveway. Since Sam had got his new car he thought he was really hot stuff. He was so stuck up that she made fun of him. She would pretend to be driving and put her nose in the air and say, "Hey, look at me! I'm a big shot." That really made him mad. Sam made straight As in math and planned to major in math in college. Priscilla knew that Sam could help her. She also knew he would laugh at her if she asked. What to do? She looked at her watch. If she didn't hurry she would miss her boyfriend's call.

Priscilla took a deep breath and knocked on Sam's door. No answer. She knocked again. Still no answer. She called, "Sam, are you in there?" and heard a muffled response, "Go away." "I really need to talk to you," she said. She bravely opened the door and walked in. To her astonishment her arrogant brother was sitting on his bed with his shoulders slumped, looking as if he had lost his best friend. She was so surprised that she forgot her own problem. Instead she said, "What's wrong, Sam?" "You wouldn't be interested," he mumbled. "Yes, I would," Priscilla replied. "Julie just broke up with me. She said she hated me and would never go out with me again." Instinctively, Priscilla came to her brother's defense. "How dare she talk that way to you! You are the star of the high school. You are the best basketball player and you make the best grades and you're the handsomest boy in the entire high school and . . ." Priscilla found herself rattling on and on. All at once Sam got up and gave her a hug and said, "Hey, that's enough." She looked up and saw him laughing. "You know, Sis, you're really great too!" Then Priscilla remembered what she had come to ask him. She hated to ask him now. Sam looked at her and said, "Now what's wrong with you?" She stared at the floor and said, "I really came to ask for some help in math, but I got so concerned about your problem that I forgot. Now I'm afraid you'll think I just said those things to get you to help me." Sam laughed and said, "Sis, you're the greatest. Let's see what's the trouble."

Brothers and sisters know each other so well. Even though they seldom say it, they have a deep family tie and love for each other. Brothers and sisters will respond when there is a need for help.

Don

Don had a helping and supportive family. Any member who had a problem could always depend on the others. At times they had their squabbles or fights, but that was all right.

Don was a middle child, with an older sister and two younger brothers. They all did homework after school at a long table in the breakfast area. It took longer there because of interruptions and having to stop and help each other, but it was also more fun. Since Merideth, the youngest, got home first, she had juice and snacks around the table ready for them. It was important in the family for everyone to do their part. Merideth, at six, wasn't old enough to help with the others' homework, but she could fix the juice and snacks for them.

When Don got home one day he heard loud sobbing. Following the sound, he saw Merideth crying on her bed. She had dropped the juice on the kitchen floor and broken the bottle. "Now no one will have any juice all week." She knew they could only afford one large bottle a week. Don laughed and said he would help her clean it up. "Merideth, you like to pretend. This week we will have pretend juice." By the time the others got home the kitchen was clean. Glasses of water and snacks of peanut butter stuffed in celery were at everyone's place. Don announced that the apple juice was just a little weak. Then Merideth told them what had happened. The incident became a highlight of their study times. They all remember the week they had "weak apple juice."

CHAPTER 12

Building
Self-Esteem

Self-esteem is not something you can buy at the store. It is not something you can get for a birthday present. Self-esteem is the confidence you have about yourself. It is the warm, cozy feeling you have about yourself. It is rather like having a built-in fireplace to lie in front of on a cold winter night. Other people cannot give you the built-in fireplace, but they can certainly cause the flames to burn higher or douse them with a cold blast of words. When people praise you, the flames burn higher in your inner fireplace. When people criticize you, it is like a cold blast. If the flames burn too low, it is hard to relight the fire by yourself. You may need some positive and supportive friends, parents, or teachers to help you get it burning brightly again.

Zachary

Zachary and his parents were driving home from the clinic to which his doctor had referred him for a complete evaluation. The clinic said it would be two weeks before they would have the results. It was very quiet in the car.

The school had said there was nothing wrong with Zachary but laziness. At first his parents had believed the school, which made Zachary feel worthless. He also felt angry and scared and very lonely. Finally he had told his parents how he felt. After talking it over, they made an appointment for Zachary with their family physician. Dr. Harris had been their doctor for years and knew Zachary inside and out. Zachary had always been able to talk to him. Dr. Harris had Zachary's parents wait while he checked Zachary and talked with him. Zachary told him what was happening in school, how everyone was angry with him, and how he was becoming angry with everybody including himself. He said he was spending four hours a day on homework and still getting Ds.

Dr. Harris called Zachary's parents in and talked to all three together. "I'm referring Zachary to a clinic for a complete diagnostic evaluation. I know he is a smart and capable young man. I definitely do not think he is lazy." Those words gave Zachary a warm feeling; it was good to have someone voice confidence in him again.

Finally the time came for Zachary and his parents to get the answers. The psychometrist informed them that Zachary's IQ was 125. He was above grade level in reading and mathematical skills. His problem was a mild form of apraxia, which is inability to manipulate objects in two- or three-dimensional space using his hands or other body muscles, causing poor writing skills. Students with mild apraxia do not always get into the learning disability program even though medically they have a learning disorder. Zachary's abilities in listening, oral expression, basic reading skills, reading comprehension, math calculation, and math reasoning were not affected. He knew the material. He simply had trouble putting it in written form. The specialist referred Zachary to an occupational therapist for help with his fine motor skills. She recommended that he be given a computer or typewriter on which to do his assignments. She also gave them a written report for the school, making recommendations for helping Zachary. She recommended that he be allowed to answer the essay parts of tests orally and that math problems be printed out so that he could just write the solutions.

Zachary's parents took the report to his school. His teachers were interested in having Zachary succeed and agreed to do whatever they could to help him.

You need to choose your friends wisely. We tend to become like our friends. If your friends are happy and secure, they have high self-esteem. Such people are positive and supportive of each other. They will give you positive feedback and help your inner flame to burn higher. Some people choose friends who are unhappy, always complaining and fussing. Such people have low self-esteem. They will be critical of each other and of you. You will soon have low self-esteem yourself and, in turn, find yourself critical of others.

Jenny

The telephone was ringing. Jenny knew it would be her friend Susan. Susan was always calling to ask Jenny to go somewhere with her. If Jenny didn't go Susan got mad at her. Susan told everyone that Jenny was her best friend. If Jenny went to Virginia's house, Susan would say, "I thought you were my best friend. Why did you go to Virginia's without me?" Jenny liked Susan, but she liked her other friends too. She liked the whole group of girls that ran around together. Susan was always criticizing the other girls. In fact, whenever Jenny was with any one of them alone, she was criticizing the others. Jenny knew they must criticize her when she wasn't there. They criticized all the other girls in school. Just last night Susan had said, "Did you see the weird way Mary wears her hair? She should be in the zoo!" When Jenny didn't laugh, Susan said, "What's wrong with you, Jenny? You like that kind of hairdo? Maybe you belong in the zoo too!" At that point all the other girls started laughing at Jenny. Jenny wished there was a way out, but she could not think of one.

Jenny picked up the phone, to hear her dad's excited voice. He wanted to talk to Jenny's mother, who was out. Jenny's dad said he couldn't wait; he had to tell someone. He had just received a big promotion that would require moving to another city. Would it bother Jenny to leave her friends. Jenny was dyslexic, and he knew how much she liked her teachers at this school. Jenny reassured him about leaving her school and teachers. Secretly she knew this was her answer to Susan. She had never told anyone about her feelings. Everyone thought they were the closest of friends. Jenny determined that in the new school she would choose her friends more wisely. She would look for happy people who were supportive of each other and not always criticizing.

Alex

Alex had made three touchdowns in the last football game, and everyone had cheered loudly for him. Whenever people saw him they yelled, "How's it going, Alex?" Alex felt good about himself. He always went out of his way to speak to other students. He was a leader in the high school. Everyone enjoyed being with him. He was always laughing but never laughed at other people. He was a good friend to have. Whenever anyone had a problem, they went to Alex, who always had time to listen. He didn't always have answers, but he listened and felt deeply about their problems. It helped to have someone just listen. People liked Alex because he never said anything negative. He never criticized them. He always tried to help them. His teachers liked him too. Alex felt good about himself.

One day at school Alex overheard two teachers talking about him. "You know, Alex has dyslexia. It is surprising for a special education student to be the most popular student in school." Instead of feeling devastated and ashamed, Alex felt proud. He realized that he was changing the way people thought about special education. That could help a lot of other students. It wasn't because he did anything really great. It was just because of his positive and accepting personality.

Rashaad

Rashaad's family were always critical of him. He never felt as if he did anything right. No matter what he tried, someone in his family told him he should have done it differently. Rashaad had quit trying. He knew it would be wrong.

Last night Rashaad's dad had told him to pour his sister a glass of milk. Rashaad just sat there, knowing that if he poured it, it would spill. His dad yelled at him as always, so Rashaad went to the refrigerator and got the milk. As he was about to begin pouring his mother said, "You shouldn't have had Rashaad pour that milk. He'll spill it and we'll have a mess to clean up." Sure enough, the milk came rushing out of the carton and missed his sister's glass. Milk went all over the tablecloth. Everyone started yelling, and his dad said, "Rashaad never does anything right." By the time the mess was cleaned up Rashaad was not hungry. He knew better than to say anything. Instead he just pretended to eat.

In his room that night Rashaad thought about running away. He began writing a note to his parents. In fact, he wrote several notes, but none of them seemed to say just the right words. He threw them away. He lay in bed wide awake and planned what he would do and how he would write the note in the morning. Finally he drifted off to sleep, only to oversleep and have to rush off to school without breakfast.

He was in his special education class for oral expression when the school counselor appeared and told the teacher that she needed Rashaad for the rest of the hour. Rashaad could not imagine why she would want to see him. He didn't think she even knew his name. In her office he was surprised to see his mother and father. He could see that his mother had been crying. The counselor spoke first. "Rashaad, your mother was cleaning your room this morning and found these notes in your wastebasket. She called your father, and they decided to come and talk to me. Your father and I went to high school together. He thought maybe I could help you." Rashaad could not think of anything to say. The counselor said that Rashaad had written some of his thoughts on paper because of his difficulty expressing them out loud. Rashaad's father said, "Son, maybe we have been too hard on you." His mother said to the counselor, "Rashaad knows we love him very much." Rashaad didn't say anything. The counselor took the opportunity to talk with the family about a positive attitude. She encouraged his parents not to comment on what he did wrong. That evening his parents talked with his brothers and sisters. From that time on Rashaad's family was more considerate of him. The counselor helped him learn to put his ideas and thoughts on paper. He was good at organizing his thoughts when he wrote them down. He left a note for his parents each day, telling them his feelings. He often told them how much he appreciated how nice they were to him. Rashaad was surprised at how contagious the positive attitude was. Everyone in the family began noticing the good things others did. Before long Rashaad became able to tell them how he felt. Now he has a positive and supportive home.

CHAPTER 13

Famous People

George Smith Patton (1885–1945)

George S. Patton suffered from dysgraphia, a disorder that causes a person to mix up the order of letters in written words. As a child George often made mistakes in writing, and the problem stayed with him all his life. Even so, he went on to become one of America's great military men.

During World War II Major General Patton was one of the leaders in the invasion of North Africa. His 2nd Army Corps soundly defeated the German army in Tunisia. Field Marshal Erwin Rommel was a highly respected German general. He was such a great desert fighter that he was called "the Desert Fox." He commanded the German army that held the remainder of North Africa. General Patton (by now Lieutenant General) would have to defeat Rommel if North Africa were to be freed. He did exactly that, giving Rommel the most crushing defeat of his career. Patton's tactics during that battle are still studied by students of warfare.

Later Patton led the 7th Army during the invasion of Sicily, winning tremendous victories at Anzio, Palermo, and Messina. During these battles General Patton used amphibious assault tactics, sending part of his army behind enemy lines in small boats called landing craft. His brilliant maneuvering so stunned the Germans that they retreated in confusion, leaving their weapons and supplies behind.

During the invasion of Normandy, General Dwight Eisenhower, the Supreme Allied Commander, used George Patton to confuse the Germans even further. General Eisenhower ordered Patton to stay in England during the invasion. The German High Command were convinced that only George Patton could lead such an audacious invasion. Because their spies reported that he was still in England, they believed that no action was taking place. Too late, they discovered that the invasion was under way.

After the invasion, Patton was promoted to full General (four star) and given command of the 3rd Army in Europe. Immediately he engineered a drive across Europe that absolutely destroyed his opponents. The 3rd Army moved farther and faster, liberated more cities and towns, and destroyed or captured more enemy soldiers than any army in history.

Albert Einstein (1879–1955)

Albert Einstein suffered from dysgraphia and dyslexia, a disorder that causes persons to see words and numbers backward. Despite his handicaps, he went on to become a great mathematical physicist.

This was quite a feat for a man who as a child was thought to be mentally retarded. His teachers had told his parents that he would never amount to anything. His parents, however, encouraged him to continue his studies.

In 1921 Einstein was awarded the Nobel Prize in physics for his quantum theory, which explained how light is transmitted. Having fled Nazi Germany in 1934, he became a citizen of the United States in 1940. He was almost sixty years old. He brought with him many brilliant ideas. During the next twenty-five years, he became the acknowledged scientific leader of the free world.

During World War II Nazi scientists were working on a secret project: the atomic bomb. Had either Germany or Japan been able to perfect and produce it, the Axis would have won the war. Although he was a confirmed pacifist, Einstein wrote a letter to President Franklin D. Roosevelt urging him to undertake development of nuclear power. The bomb was created that ended World War II several years earlier than most generals dreamed possible, saving thousands of both American and Japanese lives.

Einstein was most famous for his theory of relativity, which stated that time and speed are related. Einstein said that the faster an object traveled through space, the more slowly it would age. This astonished and fascinated many other scientists who had been trying to understand how mass and energy were related. Einstein developed a mathematical equation that stated the exact rate at which this would occur. The theory has proved to be true.

Einstein was also well known for his commitment to peace and justice.

Thomas Alva Edison (1847–1931)

Thomas Edison suffered from dyslexia. When he was a child no one understood dyslexia; they just knew that Thomas couldn't read well, and they decided that he wasn't very bright. Eventually, Thomas dropped out of school and got a job on a passenger train delivering newspapers.

Because Thomas had a lot of free time, he began to tinker with electrical gadgets. In time, he became the world's greatest inventor. His discoveries changed the quality of life around the world.

Edison invented the electric light bulb. His first light bulbs burned brightly, but only for an instant. He spent years searching for a material that would not burn out quickly. Eventually he discovered that the mineral tungsten was just what his invention needed. It would glow without burning away. The result is the modern light bulb.

Edison also invented the phonograph, then called "the talking voice box." In his experiments he discovered that a pointed metal object running across plastic could reproduce sounds. Because of his invention, we are now able to record any sound. Without it modern rock stars and companies like Sony, Walkman, and Pioneer would never have existed.

Edison had long been interested in electricity and wire. One day he combined both interests in a single invention: He was able to make a sound on one end of a wire and turn it into an electric impulse. When it traveled to the other end of the wire, he was able to turn it back into sound. His experiment was the basis of the modern telephone.

Ludwig van Beethoven (1770–1827)

Beethoven was dyslexic and had an attention-deficit disorder, an inability to pay attention for any length of time. His music is considered among the greatest in the world.

Born in Bonn, Germany, Beethoven started life with many things against him, things that would have made lesser young men give up their dreams. Not only did he have two learning disorders, but his father was alcoholic and seldom did a good day's work. This made it necessary for Beethoven to support his family. His mother died when he was seventeen.

Most composers spend years studying (called serving an apprenticeship) with other composers. Although Beethoven did get a chance to study under Mozart, his apprenticeship was brief. To support himself, Beethoven became a teacher of music. He taught children to read music and play instruments. During this time he also played the viola in an orchestra. Later he settled in Vienna, Austria, where he studied under Joseph Haydn. He became a great success as a pianist, but that career was cut short by his failing hearing. By the time he was thirty-one he was totally deaf.

Despite his deafness, Beethoven wrote nine great symphonies, nine other major orchestral pieces, thirty-two piano sonatas, one opera, and much other music.

Hans Christian Andersen (1805–1875)

Hans Christian Andersen's disability was dyscalculia, a mathematical disorder. Nevertheless he became a famous writer of fairy tales. His stories have been translated into almost every language in the world. In fact, only the Bible has been translated into more languages. You have probably read many of them. They include "The Red Shoes," "The Ugly Duckling," and "The Emperor's New Clothes."

Louis Pasteur (1822–1895)

Dyslexia and dysgraphia were the learning disabilities that Louis Pasteur lived with. Even with these limitations, he became one of the world's greatest scientists. His work influenced the fields of industry, medicine, and chemistry.

One of Pasteur's most important discoveries was that many diseases come from germs, which invade and multiply in the body. He also discovered that a preparation of weakened germs injected into the body would provide immunity to the actual disease. This technique, vaccination, has saved millions of lives.

Another brilliant discovery of Pasteur's was that living organisms come only from other living organisms. This opened a whole new field that came to be called bacteriology.

Still another amazing discovery of Pasteur's was that heat killed the germs that caused wine and milk to deteriorate or spoil. Later, this idea was used to "pasteurize" milk and beer.

It is difficult to estimate the long-range effects of Pasteur's work, because they are still being felt in the modern world. The Pasteur Institute, founded in his honor in Paris in 1888, is still a major world center for the study of disease.

The examples given so far have been of people in history. Let us look now at people making major contributions in the world today. Bruce Jenner is dyslexic but has won five gold medals in Olympic track and field events. Football star Dexter Manley is a top athlete even though he is learning disabled. Cher has dyslexia, dyscalculia, and attention deficit disorder. She has achieved fame as a singer and actress. Henry Winkler ("The Fonz" from the

"Happy Days" television show) is a popular actor and an accomplished director in spite of problems with dyslexia and dysgraphia. Whoopi Goldberg has attention deficit disorder but is an award-winning actress and comedienne. Actor Tom Cruise has also achieved greatness but is dyslexic.

In the business world, people like Paul Orfalea, founder of Kinko's Copy Centers, have overcome their learning disabilities to be successful. Mr. Orfalea has reading problems and considers himself mechanically inept. At an early age, his parents offered his siblings $50 to teach him the alphabet. He knew that his problems in reading and his mechanical awkwardness would make it hard for him to succeed in the business world. So early he set his sights on being his own boss.

When he was 22, Mr. Orfalea opened a small shop near his college that sold copies and school supplies. He named the store "Kinko's," a nickname he had acquired because of his curly hair. Today more than 17,000 people are employed in 725 Kinko's. In the future, Mr. Orfalea plans to expand into video-conferencing and other new business technology.

Thomas H. Kean is learning disabled but has achieved great success. In spite of his disability, he earned a B.A. degree from Princeton University, a master's from Columbia University, and went on to earn a Ph.D. He made a fortune in investments and was governor of the state of New Jersey from 1982 to 1990. He is currently president of Drew University, Madison, New Jersey.

Learning disabilities can prevent you from succeeding only if you let them. If you have a dream, follow it. Your life has all the potential and promise of any of these successful learning disabled people. Having a learning disability just means you may have to work a little harder!

For Further Reading

Osman, Betty. *Learning Disabilities: A Family Affair.* New York: Warner Books, 1985.

Rosner, Jerome. *Helping Children Overcome Learning Difficulties.* New York: Walker & Co., 1988.

Scheiber, Barbara, and Talpers, Jeanine. *Unlocking Potential: College and Other Choices for Learning Disabled People.* Bethesda, MD: Adler & Adler, 1987.

Skyer, Regina, and Skyer, Gill. *What Do You Do After High School?* Rockaway Park, NY: Consultation Center, 1986.

Slovak, Irene. *New BOSC Directory Facilities for Learning Disabled People.* Congers, NY: Bosc Publishers, 1990.

Straughn, Charles II, and Colby, Marvelle. *Lovejoy's College Guide for the Learning Disabled.* Kenmore, WA: S & S Enterprises, 1988.

Vail, Pricilla, *Smart Kids with School Problems: Things to Know and Ways to Help.* New York: New American Library, 1989.

Wallach, Geraldine, and Butler, Katherine. *Language Learning Disabilities in School-Age Children.* Baltimore, MD: Williams & Wilkins, 1983.

Yellen, Andrew, & Yellen, Heidi. *Understanding the Learning Disabled Athlete.* Springfield, IL: C. C. Thomas, 1987.

Index